MOLECULAR INVESTMENT CONSULTING FOR PHILANTHROPIES

A Holistic Approach for Nonprofit Management

by

Roger M. Matloff
Richard M. Ehrlich

Multi Tier Media
New York, New York

To Erica, the *foundation* of my life, who has taught me that giving is important, but caring is essential....

To my children, Adam and Breanne, who have *endowed* me with much pride and joy....

Roger

To my mother and father who have gifted me their time, love, compassion for others and values.

To my family, Ilene, Michael and Scott, watching you give unselfishly to those in need has warmed my heart to no end.

Rick

MOLECULAR INVESTMENT CONSULTING FOR PHILANTHROPIES

TABLE OF CONTENTS

Introduction   i

Chapter 1   Molecular Investment Consulting   1

Chapter 2   Demographic Analysis   17

Chapter 3   Charity Efficiency   27

Chapter 4   Fundraising   41

Chapter 5   Fiduciary Responsibility   53

Chapter 6   Asset Allocation   67

Chapter 7   Behavioral Finance   81

Chapter 8   Blind Risk Modeling   99

Chapter 9   Investment Policy Statement   115

Chapter 10   Money Manager Selection   129

Chapter 11   Dynamic Portfolio Optimization   145

Chapter 12   Investment Program Analysis   155

Chapter 13   Nonprofit Investment   167
                       Tools & Tactics
Conclusion   191

Bibliography   193

Molecular, *adj.* 1. Having to do with a group of atoms that are bound tightly together. 2. Of or relating to simple or basic organization.

INTRODUCTION

It was more than six months after the tragedy of September 11, 2001 before we were able to return to our offices at the World Financial Center just across the Westside Highway from Ground Zero. We had both been away on family business that terrible day. Like all Americans, the events struck us to our very core, especially with the news that our firm had lost several members who'd attended a breakfast meeting at the Top of the World Restaurant.

Upon our return to New York, we were initially instructed to report to an uptown office, and our first day there we brought paper and pencils to resume our work from scratch. The World Financial Center had been constructed on ground fill from the Twin Towers and, given its proximity to such devastation and the enormous power of the destruction, there was some concern as to whether or not the building's foundation was structurally sound. So it wasn't until the spring of 2002 that we finally returned to our old offices to observe with shock what lay before us.

Prior to 9/11 the view from our windows had been the imposing Twin Towers and the complex of buildings forming the World Trade Center block; now spread below was a barren expanse. An entire city block of desolation. Nothing had prepared either of us for the emotional impact of the sight. There were no words to express what we saw and felt. Everyone in the firm knew this was the communal burial site of 3,000 souls.

By this time, the economic impact of 9/11 was making itself felt in our own business as it had throughout the Tri-State region and across America. The terrorist attack and World Trade Center destruction had come on the heels of the collapse of the stock market earlier in 2001, the greatest downturn since the Great Depression.

The first reaction of Americans to the attack had been horror followed almost immediately by the desire to give. In time, 58% of all Americans contributed to one or another of the 9/11 relief funds. It has been said that as a people we are at our best when things are at their worst, and that certainly proved to be the case in those long, emotional months. In all, Americans gave $1 billion in aid to the victims of that tragic day.

Such giving, however, had the effect of diverting substantial sums from the traditional nonprofits with which we consulted and on whose boards we served. For the two previous decades, investments in stocks, bonds and cash had resulted in an all but relentless climb of gain. In such an advantageous investment environment, endowments found little difficulty in annually distributing 5% of their investment portfolio. In fact, a large number increased the percentage of their distribution during the heady days of the last decade of the 20th Century.

Overall, nonprofit giving doubled after 1996, as assets also doubled, from $226 billion to over $500 billion. In fact, the situation was so rosy that in 1999 Congress had seriously considered increasing the percentage of mandated distribution for private foundations to 8%. As it happened, this would have taken effect just at the worst possible moment.

The average increase of the stock market over decades is 10 to 12%, so when a five-year period in the 1990s saw an explosive growth rate of 20% it should have been a cautionary tale, not justification for increasing the dispersal rate. Before Congress could act, however, the dot com bubble imploded and the stock market crashed. While this had an adverse affect on all Americans to one degree or another, it had an inordinately negative impact on nonprofits.

From the time of the collapse through the long period after 9/11, monies donated to nonprofits declined significantly. One major reason was the diversion of funds into the 9/11 charities. Though millions of Americans gave who did not usually contribute significant sums to charity, the traditional "deep pocket" philanthropists also gave in very large sums, and deservedly so, but at a cost to those organizations they usually supported.

But this wasn't the only reason for the decline in giving to nonprofits. The downturn in the stock market also adversely affected contributions. What had been capital gains – a strong source of funds for donations – overnight become capital losses. Income from investments was simply lower than it had been and the traditional pool from which to draw charitable contributions was diminished, as was the income nonprofits received from their investment portfolios.

Though unemployment was high across the country at this time, New York City and its environs were the most seriously impacted. And this was another reason for the decline. Many of those who traditionally gave found their adult children suddenly out of work and felt it wise to retain their resources until the situation improved.

Corporate malfeasance was also dominating the financial headlines, and there was a change in the nature of the demographics of wealth. Government giving to nonprofits had been on the decline for two decades and was certain to continue that way. Even volunteerism, that most American of contributions to charity, was steadily decreasing as it had over the last few decades, largely as a byproduct of two-wage-earning families.

Tax laws were also changed so that dividend-paying stocks were now advantageous to hold. Previously, such stock was often donated to endowments. A lower capital gains tax rate had reduced certain charitable motivations, as did changes in state estate taxes. And to assist in the recovery, the Fed reduced interest rates to a 45-year low, stimulating the economy but also depressing the income from the bond portfolios that endowments, charities and nonprofits maintained, as well as the portfolios of those who traditionally gave.

There were other reasons for decreased charitable activity, one being the Patriot Act, which placed greater scrutiny on nonprofits, since it appeared some had been used to direct money for terrorist acts. And there was the war itself. Many previous donors simply felt that during an uncertain time it was better to retain assets.

All of this, and more, had a debilitating impact on nonprofits. As a consequence, some closed their doors, and many others were forced to lay off employees, which adversely affected fundraising. A few were compelled to merge, having the consequence of still more layoffs. Increasingly, every nonprofit found itself in competition within the same pool of traditional donors.

While today's typical nonprofit is growing, it is not growing at a rate necessary to meet the demands placed on a charity. The basic principle of nonprofits – to provide the same or an increasing level of mission support in the future – is under assault. In the face of this new reality, nearly every nonprofit is rethinking and retooling its formula for calculating its mission distribution policy.

Given the nature of our profession, we have experienced these changes and the new world of nonprofits firsthand. We are both First Vice Presidents and Institutional Investment Management Consultants for a major investment banking firm.

We assist various organizations with their asset management and philanthropic consulting needs. In helping us author this book, Joshua Jespersen took on the task of research assistant and contributed to the book's breadth of topics. He has years of experience with research and analysis in nonprofit investment consulting. Josh also designed, and continues to develop, new models and analyzes tactics which are currently in use by nonprofit investment management consultants at the head of their field in the industry. Special thanks go to Richard Slutzky, a Vice President and Senior Philanthropic consultant with a major national trust company, who was instrumental in guiding this project and providing special assistance to us.

In addition to our work as consultants, we serve on endowment boards and give of our time and income to worthy causes. But the changes we now witnessed were new to us and required that we rethink the traditional role of investment consultant to nonprofits. From that came a new methodology, Molecular Investment Consulting, a holistic approach to the entire eleemosynary field. What we determined was that nonprofits must increasingly operate in the fashion of for-profit companies if they are going to survive and fulfill their missions.

In this first decade of the 21st century, during these difficult times, it is not enough for a consultant to take the money of an endowment and invest it. That is simply too narrow a focus since nonprofits have so many greater needs. In consideration of changed circumstances, nonprofits should view their service providers in a different light and have a superior set of expectations. What they require is a broader array of services that address their ongoing, as well as their new, urgent needs.

What is needed are consultants who understand nonprofits and their overarching needs; consultants who can help structure an investment portfolio in this new, less predictable market; consultants who understand how money is raised and how to raise it, who can perform the necessary demographic studies and uncover a new class of donors; and someone who can improve efficiency of the nonprofit and help in planting seeds for future harvest.

One of the key realities of the future is that it will be

increasingly difficult to spend money to grow. For many nonprofits, caught between their giving needs and greatly reduced contributions, the response is in effect to burn down the house around them just to keep warm, ushering in their own eventual demise.

What we offer is an integrated, seamless approach to the current reality. What we have learned is that every nonprofit has its own unique DNA. They may look much the same, appear to be very similar in the essentials, but there exist significant differences. It is in understanding and capitalizing on those differences that the solution to the current impasse lays.

Traditionally there are four areas of asset-management consulting for nonprofits. These are:

- The Investment Policy Statement
- Asset allocation
- The manager search and selection
- Reporting

But within and beyond these lies a far greater world which we've come to identify and understand. Equally essential to any nonprofit is an analysis of who gives and why, the degree of investment risk a board is willing to assume, the creation of a dynamic tactical asset-allocation modeling tool, an analysis of charity efficiency, ongoing fiduciary training, and an understanding of behavioral finance. Each area can be examined and understood separately, but each serves in combination, forming in effect a molecule – a molecule combined with others to create the distinct DNA of the endowment, charity and nonprofit.

We have named the advisors who can accomplish this Molecular Consultants because we understand the needs of nonprofits down to their institutional molecular level. It is a specialized field, one very different and far more demanding than that of the traditional investment advisor.

Through its attention to what appear to be diverse details and its understanding of their application, Molecular Investment Consulting can change the very ground on which any nonprofit stands. It will cause boards to examine themselves and their nonprofit in new, more productive ways. It will greatly improve efficiency and fundraising. It will bring to any nonprofit the kind of focus for-profit companies are compelled to have by the nature of the competing marketplace – because the new reality is that they are no longer that different.

Roger M. Matloff
Richard M. Ehrlich

Having, first, gained all you can, and secondly, saved all you can, then give all you can.

– John Wesley

1.
MOLECULAR INVESTMENT CONSULTING

Because of nonprofits we are a better country. Threatened environmental areas have been preserved, the homeless and hungry have been sheltered and fed, crippling diseases have been cured, animals are safer and better treated, and social, cultural and artistic endeavors have been advanced and preserved, to name just a few ways nonprofits have made us better.

The development and evolution of American philanthropy is the envy of the world, and deservedly so. According to recent statistics, in America one million charities and nonprofits support more than half of all hospitals, 58% of social service providers, 46% of all colleges and universities, 87% of libraries, and 86% of museums and public gardens. Altogether nonprofits comprise 10 major categories comprising 26 groups with over 600 subsets. Valued at $621.4 billion in 1996, the nonprofit sector of the American economy employed 10.2 million workers, utilized the services of 5.7 million volunteers and constituted 6.2 % of the national income.

Such unselfish giving, on so vast a scale, is without equal in any time or anywhere else in the world. Significantly, American contributions to the victims of 9/11 and those for the survivors of Hurricanes Katrina and Rita in 2005 were as unselfish as those we gave to alleviate the suffering of the South Asia tsunami in 2004.

American Philanthropy

This generosity has its origins in our Judeo-Christian religious tradition, as well as in the unique history of our nation. The first American settlements were far from the mother country, distant even from one another and largely lacking formal government. These communities were compelled by circumstances, but also by inclination, to unite to satisfy local needs, such as the building of churches and schools. "Barn raisings," in which the local farmers gathered to join together to help in building the essential structures for new couples, were routine. This experience, plus the fact that so many early settlements were religious in nature, set the precedent for our tradition of charity and individual efforts to promote the common good.

The Frenchman, Alexis de Tocqueville, in his book *Democracy in America* wrote in 1835, "In no country in the world do the citizens make such exertions for the common weal." Andrew Carnegie, who acquired an enormous fortune in steel, was by 1901 devoting himself totally to philanthropy, which he said was the responsibility of every wealthy individual. He took seriously his famous saying, "The man who dies rich, dies disgraced." By the time of his death, Carnegie had given away 90% of his fortune. He, John D. Rockefeller, and others established America's first private, grant-giving philanthropies.

In 1914, Frederick H. Goff established the Cleveland Foundation, our nation's first community foundation. It was quickly followed by others and just 16 years later, 21 cities had community foundations with assets exceeding $100,000. Today, there are some 600 community foundations possessing assets in excess of $25 *billion*.

The advent of the personal income tax in 1913, followed by the decision four years later that individuals could take a tax deduction for charitable giving, was a tremendous spur to charitable contributions. During World War I, Americans gave the Red Cross more than $400 million, an enormous sum in pre-inflation dollars.

During the Depression the national government assumed a role in giving it has never entirely relinquished, though its focus has altered decade to decade. Money was distributed to antipoverty and civil rights efforts, to job training programs and other social efforts.

As millions of Americans found themselves subject to the income tax for the first time during World War Two, and given the patriotic spirit of the era, charitable contributions increased fivefold from 1939 to 1945. Since then it has continued to increase. So rapid and widespread has been the growth of nonprofits that today there are over 22,000 professional fundraisers.

The Evolving Nature of Philanthropy

One of the most significant changes in nonprofits has been the recognition by donors of the need for broad-based non-governmental solutions to persistent needs. There is an increasing recognition that giving to an immediate need is usually not a long-term or systemic solution. For example, we can give a dollar every day to the man we pass holding the "Will Work for Food" sign or we can elect instead, or in addition, to give to a community organization serving the needs of the homeless.

There are still many who are inclined to romanticize the role of geographically local independent nonprofits, believing them to be better focused, more flexible, faster and more enjoyable with which to engage. A small, local group is viewed as less top-heavy in administration, more responsive to donor direction; in general more personal and less institutional in its approach. And in some cases this is true.

But the 21st century is rapidly moving us away from the geographic community. We often have more in common with peers and colleagues living throughout our nation than we do those residing in our surrounding area. We maintain contact by telephone and the Internet; we gather information from the media as well as from a wide range of specialized venues. The needs we desire to meet are known to exist nearly everywhere, the causes about which we care are not limited to the city or county in which we live and work.

This change has come about through the development of our national transportation and communications systems and because of the increasing mobility of our population. We are born in one place, raised in two others, attend college in a fourth, and follow our career in three others. Our family is widely scattered and our charitable impulses are motivated by needs we see everywhere we have lived and traveled. What was once our small town has become our national community. For this and other reasons, we recognize the need for larger organizations, for alliances and collaborations that will put our contributions to the most effective use.

This natural progression from private charitable acts to the concept of collaborative effort through charitable organizations creates its own new requirements and realities. Can the charity be trusted? Is it efficient in its use of contributions? Does it support programs that truly address a need? These questions, along with other needs, have resulted in the increased role of professionals in assuring that the compassionate impulse in action is well served.

Some 20 years ago research identified the four stages of the charitable impulse:

- Charitable values developed through the influence of our culture, religion and immediate family.
- These values are further developed through parables, morality tales and institutions such as school and church.
- These values are engaged when we witness need, are exposed to a charity or are otherwise motivated to

act.
- Finally, we expand our personal experience and consider options other than personal philanthropy.

The consequence of this natural progression is often to assist or to contribute to charities and nonprofits.

Philanthropy Today

The nonprofit sector performs a number of vital and useful services which can be roughly organized into four sections:
- Providing conduits for the development and cultivation of public and civic values.
- Creating networks of "social capital" which support a civil society.
- Participating in and improving democratic policies.
- Increasing society's ability to realize individual potential and alleviating human misery.

Society is influenced both by what are called hard- and soft-power. "Hard-power" is defined as the military or economic force used to accomplish an objective. "Soft-power" is the ability to exert influence through the flow of information, with social, cultural and moral messages, and from relationships created through charitable acts. Hard-power can be described as compelling or pressuring others to do what you want, while soft-power is influencing others to want those things you desire.

Certain individuals such as the Dalai Lama, Nelson Mandela or Pope John Paul II exemplify, or have exemplified, the concept of soft-power. But soft-power comes not just from individuals; it can also be the result of organizations. In particular, it is the objective of nonprofits. They provide hope in the face of despair, opportunities for healing or a meaningful solution. They give purpose to the disadvantaged, and provide positive direction, and even bring about meaningful change, in underdeveloped political and educational systems.

One effect of nonprofits is to bring people together. Because of their mission and how they function, they tend to cut across racial, ethnic and cultural divides to help us see our common humanity. Many of the world's problems cannot be solved by governments. Never before have nonprofits been positioned as they are today. It has been postulated, and certainly appears to be true, that we are about to enter a new, and better, era of soft-power.

The incredible truth is that American nonprofits are poised to face the greatest challenge of their existence. Changing times and priorities mean that Americans are participating less in civic organizations and volunteering less frequently. But what has appeared to be a bleak picture is quite the opposite and the challenge is one that any sector would welcome.

It may be very possible that a new golden age of philanthropy is about to dawn. John Havens and Paul Schervish of Boston College in their recent study estimate that no less than *$41 trillion* will be generationally trans-ferred over the next 25 years. They have concluded that approximately 25% of that will be given to charity. The consequences for society, and for nonprofits, are almost incalculable.

This influx of new money is expected to change the face of nonprofit giving in a way that is unprecedented, in part because of the nature of the modern donor. Those in a position to give will tend to be activists, accustomed to seeing the results of what they do. These modern donors will treat nonprofits more like the for-profit corporations with which they have experience. They will demand account-ability and efficiency. Nonprofit behavior that was once accepted as normal and expected will be looked down upon, and long-established endowments with causes not in popular favor will likely find themselves in a very difficult position if they don't change.

For this and other reasons, engaging the next generation in supporting their mission is one of the vital roles nonprofits face. They must reach out to those they have traditionally ignored, if for no other reason than these people will possess previously unknown wealth. In so doing they must educate them about charitable giving and their own specific mission, and most must change how they conduct their affairs.

The Modern Donor

Understanding the modern donor is a vital part of future planning for any nonprofit. The time is rapidly approaching when legacy and routine donations will no longer be the most important part of fundraising.

The new donor has been the subject of extensive research, and it is well documented that he or she "wants to make a difference," to "give back" some of what the donor has earned or inherited. Studies have shown that they have a number of shared goals, most of which come from their own entrepreneurial experience or are logical extensions of it. They understand the value of giving as part of a group so they can leverage financial resources. They understand that American philanthropy has a long history and tradition, and they want to understand that and how it functions when they are making their decisions about where and how much to donate. They are willing to learn from others, from successes as well as failures, in their decision-making. In these regards, they are not all that different from the traditional donor.

The modern donor, however, is also asking for something few nonprofits are able to provide: concrete proof that contributions make a difference in their mission. A portion of this demand comes from the modern donor's own experience in business. They've invested large sums from time to time and learned from experience to insist on seeing a genuine impact from the investment. They are experienced in measuring results, seeing the effectiveness of a marketing campaign, and evaluating growth, sales or various product strategies. They have learned how to devise a strategy that can be measured in its impact. Investing resources, measuring, then determining if the goal has been achieved are skills they have finely honed in achieving business success. This is all familiar territory and it seems to them quite logical to extend it to this new world of nonprofits. And they are right to do so.

One of the reasons why the modern donor feels comfortable in demanding proof of impact is the wide range of nonprofit donation options available today. They have a number of creative investment vehicles they can employ, each offering its own distinct advantages. Choices less than a decade old are now commonplace. They can give while also benefiting in ways that reduce, eliminate or delay tax obligations.

When it comes to contributing, the modern donor may give directly to an established nonprofit, or he or she might create or enter one of the new nonprofit vehicles such as a charitable network that is a hybridized variation of existing nonprofits, structured in such a way as to require greater accountability and clear evidence of mission impact.

It is common for the modern donor to participate in several such vehicles; that is, to have, in effect, a balanced portfolio of giving just as they have one for their investments. It is quite common for such donors to create their own vehicle through which they funnel their charitable contributions.

There are several characteristics that are typical of the modern donor:

- They tend not to take advice from traditional nonprofit sources.
- They rely on peers in making decisions and are more likely to seek out such a peer who is already active in philanthropy.
- They learn how to deal with this new world from their workplace experience.
- They believe in the power of networking.

- They place great reliance on technology.

Keeping this in mind, when it comes to "reaching" the modern donor there are a number of recommended steps, many of which are quite different from the traditional means of approaching a potential donor:

1. Contact them through their network, not the one you typically use.
2. Provide true stories of success as part of the educational process.
3. Have a useful Internet website.
4. Produce a book or publish articles to give your nonprofit greater credibility and to serve as a conduit for your ideas.
5. Be creative in seeking out the modern donor. They are not to be found where you usually go.

What all of this means is that you must employ new methods and new thinking in identifying and bringing into your donor pool the modern, generational donor. It may mean forming an institutional connection with his or her organization. It may mean operating in the new high technology world in ways you've never before experienced.

It is daunting, but well worth the effort. The sums involved are absolutely enormous.

The DNA of Nonprofits

The distinctive DNA of each charity or nonprofit is as unique to it as its mission, its history, its structure and each individual board member. Why a nonprofit does what it does, how it reacts in crises as well as during good times, are all vital to its success, the confidence of its donors and the financial well-being of those to whom it contributes. What is surprising is how little attention has been given historically to these distinctions.

One of the major steps a nonprofit takes is constructing

an investment strategy and putting it in writing in what is called an Investment Policy Statement, or IPS. This usually consists of listing the goals of the nonprofit, identifying the investment parameters, recognizing the risks associated with them, and setting in place the type of communication there will be between the investment consultant, the money manager and the nonprofit.

Too often, however, the IPS is created in a vacuum, lacking proper and vital groundwork. It is through such prior work that the Molecular Consultant comes to know a client well. It is imperative that he thoroughly understand the nonprofit. The situation, and the needs, are too complex for anything less.

The Molecular Consultant will hold discussions with the people who run the nonprofit and will learn what constitutes the full scope of the mission and who it is they are serving. By understanding the lifeblood of a nonprofit, that is, to grasp the unique nature of its DNA, the Molecular Consultant will come to understand the depth of the market they serve, as well as the constituency that gives them money.

Problems for a nonprofit can come from an unexpected direction. Consider what happened to the March of Dimes. The National Foundation for Infantile Paralysis came into existence in the 1930s through the efforts of President Franklin Roosevelt, who had been afflicted by the disease. By the time an effective vaccine was finally developed, more than half a million Americans, a large portion of them children, had been struck by polio. Comedian Eddie Cantor coined the phrase "March of Dimes" during a radio broadcast, urging Americans to send their dimes directly to the White House.

While the development of the vaccine in 1952 was the climax of a 20-year effort, it left the foundation in a very difficult position. Its cause was largely accomplished. Before the vaccine was developed, the March of Dimes had an enormous donor pool. Afterwards, it diminished and had to be reestablished. Aware that the primary reason for its existence was gone, in 1958 the March of Dimes began funding research and innovative programs to save babies from birth defects, premature birth and low birth weight. All the while it continued its efforts to expand vaccination worldwide, and by 2001 the World Health Organization reported just 480 cases of polio on the entire planet.

The Demographic Analysis

When you understand your potential contributing pool, you are in position to anticipate future giving in unique and potentially highly productive ways. It is for this reason that Molecular Consultants conduct a broad-based demographic analysis. It does not focus on details of those who already give, such as specific ages and how much they donate. The analysis is conducted into the much greater *potential* pool and asks the question: How many others are there who might give?

It is surprising how often nonprofits focus only on the size and nature of the pool from which they already receive contributions. The development director usually knows if the pool of contributors is relatively young and increasing in number, or if it's elderly and declining. He or she understands which parts of the pool give the most.

Though many nonprofits grasp the primary reasons for donations, more often than not they do not know the deeper motivations for charitable giving. Understanding the demographic characteristics of those who could potentially contribute, along with their attitude towards charitable giving, their values and beliefs, their perceptions of what it is they can participate in is essential, as it provides insight into what kind of information is most useful to contributors. It also allows you to understand those vital issues about which you must be concerned to increase donations.

Understanding the broader demographics of your donor pool can also help in telling you how to invest your money.

If you are able to gather a very large amount of money through donations you can invest differently than if you are receiving very little. The direction contributions will take in the future, up or down, will also affect how you invest.

You also ought to know if the need base of the organization is expanding dramatically or decreasing. This kind of knowledge will help the development director and those responsible for raising money. Such is the value of a demographic analysis.

Blind Risk Modeling

In traditional investment consultation, an early step is establishing an asset allocation model. This is intended to help you blend different classes of assets – say stocks, bonds, cash, and alternative investments – to provide the highest rate of return with the least amount of risk. In the 1950s the concept of examining three key variables to determine a superior model was developed and received wide acceptance. These are:

1. ***Rate of Return Expectation.*** What do you expect to earn from stocks, bonds or alternative investments? This will bring into view all investment vehicles which may be able to suit your return needs.
2. ***Correlation between Asset Classes.*** What is the interaction and relationship of the various vehicles in which you may invest? For example, the inverse relationship between stocks and bonds. Understanding the correlation among all of your possible investments will allow you to gain a better grasp of how you can diversify.
3. ***Risk Assessment.*** What is the risk tolerance of your nonprofit? How much downward movement can your nonprofit handle before it will no longer tolerate losses?

As for the last, it is our experience that the risk of any

organization is in most cases a compilation of the risk tolerance of the individual board members. In Blind Risk Modeling, the Molecular Consultant determines each member's own risk tolerance, and then weighs it accordingly. While it is true that the sum can be greater than the parts; that is, the combined knowledge and experience of each board member can create a process superior to any single individual, it is also true that the lemming factor exist that is, groups have a tendency to rush over the cliff in unison. The key to understanding the predisposition of any board is what comes from Blind Risk Modeling.

Dynamic Modeling Tool

No investment portfolio is ever static. For that reason they must always be adjusted to reflect the market and the needs of the nonprofit. When it is necessary to rebalance a portfolio, the Molecular Consultant does not do it blindly, which frankly is the most common method. It even has a name: Static Revision. If the IPS formula is 50% stock and 50% bonds, the traditional investment consultant thoughtlessly rebalances to that.

What this approach doesn't take into consideration are relative values. The fact is that the market is a tool and isn't always rational in how it functions. A herd mentality can possess investment, and certain classes of vehicles [meaning securities of all types including stocks, bonds and alternative investments] can have greater cachet at one time than at another. The result is that some investment vehicles can be overvalued, while others may be undervalued. Knowing which is which is not the result of some gut response; it is the consequence of a detailed, established and accepted process for making the determination, one in which the Molecular Consultant is well versed.

Charity Efficiency Analysis

How much does it cost nonprofits to raise a dollar? That is often the most important question of all. One charity might spend a few pennies per dollar raised, while another could spend most of the donation. Fundraising can become very expensive and not as productive for established nonprofits.

As part of the evaluation, Molecular Consultants will perform a satellite fundraising analysis; that is, they identify those who might have an interest in what the nonprofit does, but for some reason don't give to it. The Molecular Consultant will host a fundraiser targeting just such potential modern donors who've never given money to this particular nonprofit with an eye to eventually expanding the donor pool. They may not get much the first time, but the idea is to plant the seed for the future, to draw them closer into your donor pool.

Fiduciary Training

Because of 9/11 everything has changed, not just for America in general and the world at large, but for all financial institutions. We now have the Patriot Act. The new reality is to determine where money comes from and where it is going. At about the same time, Congress passed the Sarbanes-Oxley Act which established new standards of financial conduct for corporate America. Eliot Spitzer, the New York state Attorney General has also subjected nonprofits to enhanced scrutiny, as has the Better Business Bureau. Examined now are compensation packages, the governance of the board members, and many other practices that were previously ignored.

As a result, board members are more aggressively scrutinizing the nonprofit, demanding proof that it is being properly run. They want to know the degree of their personal fiduciary responsibility and exposure. For this and other reasons, it is important to know how the nonprofit is run.

Every board member has a fiduciary responsibility. This means many things, but one of them is that if things go wrong the member can suffer adverse consequences. On the other hand, if things go well, while the member might garner accolades, he or she gains nothing financially.

Proper training and education in their board role is important and increasingly vital. Such a program provided by the Molecular Consultant also helps in attracting new board members because they know they will learn what is necessary to ensure that the entire organization is in compliance with the law and regulations.

Behavioral Finance

Individuals like to believe they are not influenced in dollar issues by their own psychological makeup, but that is not the case. We are all influenced, to one degree or another, by our character and those complex psychological factors that drive us. It is possible to suppress our basic impulses, but in most cases that results in a counter psychological response of which we are generally unaware. We are complex organisms and rarely have a full grasp of those internal forces that drive us. No matter how much we understand something intellectually, our response will nearly always have a psychological underpinning.

The psychology of any board in determining an investment strategy is the result of those psychological factors that influence each board member. This is one of the most powerful reasons for the need of a Molecular Consultant.

There are other important issues but these are the major ones about which each nonprofit should be concerned, though there are a number of valuable and necessary subsets. The Molecular Consultant will work in collaboration with asset managers, the investment committee, the development director and the board to provide an integrated approach. He will help your nonprofit raise capital more effectively, and assist you in making superior investment decisions, while at the same time assessing the transparency of operations the government and the modern donors demand and expect.

2.
THE DEMOGRAPHIC ANALYSIS

In few areas of society is there greater misunderstanding than when it comes to charities and charitable giving. Who gives, and why, is often the source of confusion and misunderstanding, not just for the average individual, but very often for charities and nonprofits. An important function of the Molecular Consultant is to provide the valuable information about your donors that you may currently lack.

Corporations, Foundations and the Individual

It is commonly held that most nonprofits receive the vast majority of their donations from corporations and foundations. The truth is very different. Foundation and corporate giving today comprises just over 12% of all charitable contributions in America. The balance comes directly from individuals, some by bequest, but most from living donors. What is surprising isn't the relative obscurity of this reality, but rather the great number of nonprofits that focus almost exclusively on corporations and foundations in their fundraising activities.

Though foundations and corporations give a much

smaller percentage, during the 1980s that giving increased threefold. During the same time, however, there were reductions in government funding to nonprofits as well as a significant increase in the numbers of endowments created for specific needs. As a result, the competition for foundation and corporate donations has never been keener.

On top of this, corporate and foundation giving tends to focus on specific activities and identified programs. That is, their money comes with more restrictions than the average donation. It can also be a one-time grant for a specified number of years. This can be limiting to many nonprofits, which is why individual donations are doubly important. The situation is compounded by corporate mergers. The new entity that emerges tends only to give to nonprofits the amount one of them gave previously, so the result is a net decline in the contribution.

For all the attention corporations and foundations receive, the long-term health and vitality of nonprofits stems in large part from their effective targeting of individual giving. For that reason, a significant amount of time and effort should be devoted to the individual donor, and the successful charity will develop effective strategies to attract modern donors to replace those who fall away or to increase the donor pool.

The Evolving Donor Pool

At its core, fundraising consists of asking people to give to a certain cause. This is the case whether you approach an individual, corporation or foundation. Though there is the tendency when approaching a foundation or corporation to consider this a form of "business-to-business" contact, the reality is that you are always dealing directly with people. Motivating and exerting influence over those capable of giving what you require, or those who are in control of the giving decision process, is the essence of successful fundraising.

To accomplish this you must understand your potential donors. Who are they? Why do they give? To what cause or causes would they like to give? Surprisingly, these are not questions very often asked, let alone answered, by large numbers of nonprofits.

The donor pool is always changing; it is never stagnant. Even if a pool remains fixed in terms of donor numbers, they are changing, aging every year, with altered financial circumstances, with new or refocused interests. Take one nonprofit with which we worked. For decades it has depended on the generosity of immigrants from a certain region of Europe. They anticipated the rate of giving would continue, especially since a portion of that population had developed a much higher than average net worth. In making this assumption they were depending on their general understanding of their donor pool taken as a whole.

Our demographic study, however, revealed that the most affluent portion of their potential donor pool did not give to that charity or one with their mission. Not at all. There were historic and cultural reasons why this was the case, reasons the charity did not appreciate or understand. The reality was that those in the pool who *did* give were dying every day and not being replaced.

Such a situation is not unique from our experience. Nonprofits often depend on contributions from a donor pool about which their knowledge is either incomplete or essentially false.

The Impact of Demographics

At their conception, nonprofits see a need. They identify a pool from which to draw donations and another group or groups to which they will make contributions to serve the need. Over time, new needs are embraced or service to the existing ones is expanded, and the funding of a worthy cause increases. The demand for more contributions places constant pressure on fundraising.

While the need is typically never ending, there does come a time, for most nonprofits, when the pool from which they receive donations no longer expands or begins to diminish with the death of past donors and the changing priorities of those who remain.

Consider the example of a common charity with a demographic issue. Their mission is to help the population in the country of origin for its pool of contributors. Those who immigrated to the United States still have relatives in their land of birth and as their economic circumstances here improve they give to the charity. Over the years, many of them begin to do quite well financially and they give even more. In time, their adult children give. But eventually the connection to the "old country" becomes distant as the family moves into its third and fourth generations. All the while those who immigrated have died off and are not replaced by significant numbers of new immigrants. Contributions simply dwindle. This is the life cycle of many nonprofits and in that regard all of them tend to face the same reality.

One of those realities is that often the cost of raising funds begins to rise as more pressure is placed on the long-established donor pool. Increased mailings and/or telephone solicitations, more events, all cost money, usually with a lower rate of donations. Efforts to reach out to others beyond the traditional donor pool tend to be expensive and the efforts are usually haphazard, and not sustained over time.

The ethnic makeup of America is changing. That has always been the case and will continue to be for the foreseeable future. Twenty-five percent of the American population today is composed of those with either Hispanic or African-American ancestry. The percentage of Hispanics is projected to increase and in the immediate decades the proportion of the population of Asian ancestry is also going to increase significantly. To what nonprofits will these ethnic groups give? How will their numbers affect the amount of giving and the target of that giving by the rest of the population?

The implications for nonprofits of the evolving and ever-changing American population should be self-evident. People give to those causes with which they identify; they give where they think it will make a difference. Charities and nonprofits must approach those non-traditional groups which are forming an ever greater part of our society, they must set in place programs with which they can identify, they must demonstrate that they care and want to help.

The Looming Windfall

Another profound change is taking place as concerns the nature of American wealth. Not only are trillions of dollars about to change generational hands, but the greater percentage of those who will come into this wealth will be women. These will be women unlike their mothers and grandmothers. They will be accustomed to careers, women who have handled their own investments and finances for decades, women accustomed to making their own decisions. In addition, women will be taking control of family businesses in far greater numbers and will be elected to manage family foundations. Women with ever-growing financial power are poised to become the dominant force in American nonprofits.

This is simply a reflection of the evolving role of women in our society. More women, for example, are enrolled in our universities and colleges, and, of course, more women than men receive university degrees. Women will continue to increase their presence in non-traditional professions and in many of them, law to name but one, they will become predominant.

So it isn't just that the American population is getting older, and richer, it's *who* is getting older, living longer, and becoming very much richer.

The graying of America, that is the age demographic, will also have a profound impact on charitable giving. The fastest growing segment of our population are those 85 years of age and older. In fact, before long there will be 100,000 Americans older than 100 years. To gain access to this increasing percentage of the population nonprofits must act now.

One significance of these seniors becoming older is that they will almost certainly have greater concern for their health, for their ability to pay for medical care and for their own well being. The result might be a lowered commitment to charitable giving as they retain funds to see to their medical needs. For this reason, it may very well be that this group will be more receptive to charitable giving through estate planning.

Another change that is taking place is the growing numbers and influence of the "baby boomer" generation. As a group they tend to hold less loyalty to certain causes and institutions than their parents and grandparents did. They are also inclined to be less trusting, to want greater account-ability and to require more detailed information as a result. They also tend to be less long-term in their expectations and want to give where they can see the money create an immediate change.

Understanding Those Who Give

Why people give to charity is complex, more complex than most realize. Understanding who gives and why is vital to the success of any charity or nonprofit. Donors are driven by both external pressure and internal forces. It is generally accepted that most donors give for a wide range of reasons, many of which oscillate and can be difficult to identify. They can be motivated by religion, ethnicity, race, pride, guilt, by their peers or for any one, or combination of many, other factors. The evolution of the established donor pool can be subtle and quite sophisticated. It is often useful for an experienced outsider to take a fresh look at those who give.

Charities and nonprofits are continuing organizations

like any corporation. Institutional thinking is the norm and every such organization has certain beliefs, even myths, about itself. These evolve over the years and are presented as fact to those who come onboard later. Certain assumptions which were likely true many years before persist, but often those assumptions are no longer accurate. These have a tendency to muddy reality and to implant misconceptions. Because of this, and other reasons, often nonprofits do not understand as completely as they could the nature of those who give and why they are motivated.

For management purposes, research has reduced charitable motivations to three broad themes. They are:

- A sense of personal responsibility to others.
- Relationships with others.
- Personal benefits from giving, such as recognition, reduced taxes, pleasing an employer.

Each of these can be broken into component parts and form a complicated tapestry of drives and inducements. They can be self-evident or profoundly concealed.

One of the most dominant and obvious factors in determining who gives is socio-economic status. In other words, those with immediate financial concerns give less than those who are more affluent. For example, not surprisingly, those who itemize on their tax returns give four times as much as those who don't.

You also want to know which parts of your pool contribute the greatest amounts and why they give. You need to know how many you can reasonably touch, and how much you can expect to raise from them. In this way you can more accurately assess how much more they might be willing to contribute, or determine if they would be receptive to including your nonprofit in their bequest.

Many emigrants to America come from countries where there is no history of philanthropy. The government is expected to have programs for charity or it is the church that takes care of the poor. The concept of charitable giving can be very new to these people. Finding a way to reach them, to educate them and pull them into your pool has never been more important. All these, and many, many others are questions that must be answered if you are to properly and fully understand the pool from which you receive your financial support.

With this kind of information and more, it is often possible, with certain caveats, to project future giving patterns. You can know today how much your nonprofit will receive from your existing donor pool. Such information is invaluable in planning for both your long-term and short-term future. But you must be cautious when making projections because a single donor responsible for a large percentage of your contributions could die or move away and lose interest. Nothing is certain.

But such information, even with these limitations, provides you with the means to be more productive in your fundraising with your existing pool and in this way have the effect of significantly reducing costs.

Understanding Those Who Don't Give

It is generally of equal value to understand why some don't give, or perhaps more importantly, why they have stopped giving. Detailed studies have developed four common reasons:

- Individual situations.
- Communication.
- Reaction to solicitations.
- The image of the charity or nonprofit.

Evolving contrary beliefs, a dislike for certain programs, a change in an individual's personal situation, all influence the decision not to give. Failing to receive the kind of information a modern donor is looking for can also have a dampening impact on giving.

In the time of numerous telephone solicitations, many

donors felt besieged, and while the overall numbers reflected that phone banks were an effective means of fundraising, they did not reveal the extent of ill will such methods caused. In some cases donors are asked so often, or in ways which they consider to be manipulative, that they simply stop giving.

In life, reputation and image can be everything. Certainly the United Way has found that large numbers of previous donors no longer give as a direct consequence of accusations in 1992 that United Way's national leader had committed fraud, embezzlement and other misdeeds. This was quickly followed by a string of local revelations and scandals. Today, the United Way receives fewer donations, when adjusted for inflation, than it did a decade ago, even as charitable giving overall doubled. As recently as 2002, *The New York Times* reported misdeeds by the United Way. Such adverse stories only continue to harm this once-fine charity's image and adversely impact its fundraising.

In the world of charities and charitable giving, image and reputation can make or break you.

Understanding Those You Serve

It is important to understand the needs of those a nonprofit serves. In most cases, but not all, the need will grow over the years, as programs are expanded and our population increases. But that is not always the case, as in the example of the March of Dimes. Future needs will affect fundraising and investment requirements. So understanding the direction and degree of future growth in those programs supported by a nonprofit is vital, and often overlooked.

Demographics and Investing

Once the Molecular Consultant has helped you under-stand your demographics, you will find that you also possess valuable information on how to invest your portfolio. If you know that contributions have plateaued, or will even diminish a bit based on your new understanding of your donor pool, then you will invest your money one way. If you know that you will have a steadily rising rate of contributions, you will invest it another. The key is the demographic analysis of those who give and could potentially give.

The same concept applies to those who receive your assistance. If the need is relatively stable, you will invest one way. If it is certain to rise, then you invest another.

Such demographic knowledge is invaluable to those responsible for managing the direction of any nonprofit, and is equally important to those responsible for your fundraising. All of this, and more, falls within our demographic analysis. The information acquired by the Molecular Consultant contributes greatly to the effectiveness of the nonprofit in fulfilling its mission.

3.
CHARITY EFFICIENCY

Modern donors are already giving, and in the years to come will give ever increasingly, but only after a much deeper analysis than has occurred historically. The modern donor also tends to give large blocks of capital to a small number of nonprofits, rather than smaller amounts to a larger number. They want to make an impact and want to see that their contributions are causing that impact.

If you are going to raise this new, generational money then you must understand this kind of thinking. To prosper, charity efficiency is key. When you make a presentation and can say, and honestly show, that a significant percentage of donations goes to your mission, not to inefficient fundraising or administration, it is an appeal that will be well received and one that could be key to future growth.

Persistent Inefficiency

Like every human business creation, any successful nonprofit can become sluggish and less responsive over time. We all tend to become set in our ways, and little by little lose focus and become occupied with non-essentials. It is simply human nature. Nonprofits are typically focused on the greater good and on fulfilling their mission. The day-to-day details of their operation often don't receive the attention they deserve.

In the last two decades there have been tremendous improvements in office efficiency for for-profit corporations, improvements made possible by substantial investments in infrastructure and technology. Few nonprofits find themselves in a position to be able to make such capital outlays and as a result are often compelled to operate in less efficient ways.

Additionally, there is a tendency for nonprofits to believe that optimal efficiency doesn't matter, that in the grand scheme of their affairs, it simply isn't that important. They believe they are engaged in a great cause and that a certain level of inefficiency is to be expected and will be tolerated. Because of this attitude we all lose.

One group of experts estimates that nonprofits could save *$100 billion* by changing how they operate. This sum represents 13% of the $800 billion spent each year by American nonprofits and is four times greater than all annual charitable contributions by foundations. To accomplish this, the most poorly performing half of nonprofits need only operate with the efficiency of the better performing half. Not surprisingly, the CEOs of some of our largest nonprofits deny the accuracy of this estimate.

One means of identifying the disparity in efficiency is to compare the gaps in efficiency among local branches of national nonprofits. Performing much the same function with the same mission, you'd expect they'd be quite similar, and you'd be wrong. For example, there is a 36% gap in measured efficiency among local United Ways, and an 87% gap among like local foundations. An efficiency gap of 39% exists among symphonies and one of 65% exists in similar educational scholarship programs. Such extremes defy logic, especially to potential donors.

Charity efficiency matters to nonprofits because it matters to those who donate. More significantly those in control of the estimated $41 trillion which will be generationally transferred over the next 25 years will demand charity efficiency in the nonprofits to which they give. They come from a generation that has witnessed many scandals in charities as well as on Wall Street. They've learned not to trust, and along with results, they expect transparency and accountability. The days when any charity can remain static and function as it always has are long gone.

Some years ago, in many New York City apartment buildings, a blue recycling basket was placed near the mailboxes. Over time those boxes have increased in size. A significant portion of what fills them are the unopened solicitation letters of nonprofits. There's a lesson in this. What was once an effective technique for fundraising is today far less effective. There are many reasons, one of which is less automatic trust of such solicitations.

Reports of poor charity efficiency appear routinely in the national media. In the coming years, charity efficiency will become more and more significant to the success and survival of every American charity.

Consider it this way: The worth of any charity or nonprofit is determined by the success of meeting its charitable mission and by the low cost of its own fundraising and administration. This is, in part, because the key question for most potential modern donors is whether or not the money they are considering giving will be put to a good and worthy use, and not squandered in inefficient fundraising and rising administrative costs.

Worthiness

Considering charity efficiency for nonprofits is akin to determining profits for a traditional for-profit corporation. The reality is that, relatively speaking, nonprofit executives are not especially well compensated and they do not work in lavish offices. But that is not the image presented over television when a nonprofit scandal erupts. A very different impression is conveyed and no one wants to give a dollar to a worthy cause only to learn from the extreme examples reported in the media that 90 cents of it went to pay "inflated salaries" or to maintain a lavish lifestyle in "opulent" offices or to compensate a telemarketer. The point of giving is to make a difference for those who are intended to receive assistance, not to support a costly infrastructure, cadre of bureaucrats or obnoxious fundraisers. For many potential donors this is the single most important issue.

In some cases, especially for those charities and nonprofits of long standing with well-established income streams, it can be easy to slip into complacency and allow overhead and fundraising costs to grow disproportionately. A traditional, very successful charity can become a victim of its own success and reputation.

The costs of fundraising also tend to increase over time. One reason is that the original pool of donors often stops growing and reaches a saturation point. As a result, a charity or nonprofit leans more and more heavily on those who have always given, with less productive results in too many cases.

Wages for paid staff also increase to attract better more qualified candidates, all products needed for fundraising cost more each campaign, and the price for entertainment is always rising. And on top of these are the legitimate and ever-increasing costs of administration. Keeping such costs in line is a challenge because one of the realities of all charities is that as they age they tend to become top heavy with increasingly complacent, risk-averse managers.

This is the natural evolution of nearly all human endeavors. It's why government gets bigger every year, everywhere. It's why a school district with a declining student body has an increasing number of administrators. It's why established corporations are heavy in upper management and thick with middle managers. This all too human tendency is a predicable development every charity must honestly confront if it is to prosper.

The Benefits and the Pitfalls

In considering the efficiency of the charities, nonprofits and endowments to which donors want to contribute, there are a number of factors the Molecular Consultant will consider. Charity financial reporting tends to be unclear and inconsistent, and in many cases it can be incorrect. Responsible donors will carefully examine the reporting of any charity or nonprofit to be certain it is a fit and worthy recipient.

In determining the efficiency of a charity or nonprofit, potential modern donors will also consider administrative expenses and compensation packages. The most sophisticated donors will understand there exists keen competition for key administrators, that such persons can be invaluable to a charity or nonprofit and that their services do not come cheaply.

Many charities and nonprofits are organized on the national, state or local level. Such a structure can be fertile ground for creative accounting. A sophisticated donor will understand this and examine such reporting very closely. In the event of heightened media attention to the nonprofit sector of the economy, a bright light can be shined on reporting practices that are acceptable, but misleading. The damage in such a situation, especially if the media decides to make an example of a certain charity or nonprofit, can be immeasurable in its lasting negative impact. Ask the United Way.

Determining the Scores

To evaluate and compare charities, we rely on scores that come from our impartial examination. Because of their tax status, and the realities of their situation, charities and nonprofits are in effect an open book. To maintain their tax exempt status they are required to submit a tax return, called the Form 990, to the Internal Revenue Service. You can easily examine your nonprofit's tax return at www.guidestar.org.

There are two general areas of financial health that are most closely scrutinized, and all foundations and endowments are scored in both areas. These are organizational efficiency and organizational capacity

Charity Navigator, a widely respected charity rating organization, has developed a system for scoring efficiency which many in the industry, as well as potential donors, have come to rely on. It and other rating organizations employ certain financial ratios or performance categories to rate every charity in these two areas. In so doing, they depend on the financial information each charity lists on its tax returns or on the Internal Revenue Service Form 990.

In addition to establishing a score in each of these areas, they can also give an overall rating that depicts the charity's efficiency performance by combining the two scores. This is a form of shorthand that can be very helpful to an affluent potential donor.

Organizational Efficiency

Simply stated, efficient charities spend less money to raise more money. Another way of putting it is that efficient charities spend less on administrative costs and a higher percentage on the programs and services they support.

In general, there are four performance areas that consultants scrutinize in determining the efficiency of a charity or nonprofit. A rating is established in each of these areas and from them comes a combined rating to reflect a positive or negative ratio of expenses to distribution.

These ratios are typically converted into a rating score from 0 to 10. They are also used to establish a star score, usually one to four, with four being the best. These two scores are intended to reflect a charity's efficiency in a specific category and to allow comparison with its peers.

Fundraising Efficiency

To be an effective charity, one to which the modern donor will want to give, you must be an efficient fundraiser. The amount spent to raise money must be an acceptable, even a desirable, percentage of what is ultimately collected.

Fundraising efficiency is simply how much a charity spends for each dollar collected. This is determined by dividing fundraising expenses by the total of contributions it receives as a consequence. For example, if $100,000 is spent to raise $200,000 the fundraising efficiency is $.50. But if the charity spends the same $100,000 and raises $1 million, than its fundraising efficiency is $.10.

Fundraising Expenses

While fundraising tends to be the focus of most charities, and rightfully so, raising money isn't really what they were created to do. The purpose of a charity is to support its mission; that is, support those services and programs all donors want to see helped. Maintaining a responsible cost for fundraising is vital, and an area too many charities, especially those of long standing, neglect over time. Fundraising expenses creep up and up, year after year, until one day the charity has a scandal on its hands. And it should be no surprise that unreasonable fundraising costs are often associated with conflicts of interest.

It is important to consider how much is spent on fundraising compared to how much is spent elsewhere within the charity. The rating organizations evaluate fundraising expenditures and compare them to overall spending. They establish a rating by taking the expenses and dividing them by the charity's overall expenditure. For example, if a charity spends $800,000 and raises $4.5 million from the effort, it spends 17.8% on fundraising.

Program Expenses

Charities do not exist as tax write-offs or to hold annual galas. They exist to support worthy causes that promote the social good. Most of every charity's annual budget should be given to its programs and services.

In many cases a charity spending at least 60% of its budget on programs is doing well, but the reality is even better. In fact, evaluations have determined that seven out of ten charities spend no less than 75% of their expenses on programs and services. The remaining 25% go to fundraising and administrative costs. This is a ratio about which the industry can deservedly be proud.

Again, the raters calculate a ratio which can be used to rate program expenses from one charity to another. They divide program expenses by a charity's total expenses. For example, if a charity spends $5 million on its program expenses with a total operating budget of $6 million, it spends 83% on program expenses, an excellent state of affairs.

There is a dark side here, however, that supports the most skeptical critic's doubts when it comes to some charities. The Better Business Bureau has estimated that some appeals consume 85% to 90% of the money collected. Such a figure is not unusual in far too many situations and tends to be most common when telemarketers are used. The same data revealed that 17% of charities ran a *deficit* in the previous three to five years while 8% of charities gave *less* than 60% of their budgets to programs and services.

Still, these are relatively low numbers and as should be apparent, a way exists to weed such charities out from those that perform a far more commendable service to society.

Administrative Expenses

The ratio of administrative expenses to other costs is a

matter of concern to all potential donors. A charity must have a place of business, a talented staff and skilled administrators to do well, but the costs for these must not be allowed to become disproportionate.

The same logic is followed here as previously. You take the administrative costs of a charity and divide them by the charity's total expenses. If a charity spends $400,000 in administrative costs out of total expenses of $4.7 million, it is expending 8.5% on administrative expenses, again, a very good ratio.

These ratios, and their average, determine the organizational efficiency and allow comparison of one charity to another. They can have a great deal to do with a charity's overall success. As scores are adjusted into the disadvantageous range, donors will begin to notice, and such adverse ratings will have a damaging effect on the charity and its mission. And it won't be just the administrators who pay. Those programs and services the nonprofit supports will also suffer.

In fact, rating organizations have a formula for taking these figures, comparing them one year to another and devising from that what is called a "deficit." Just as a for-profit will suffer if it finds itself in a deficit situation for any extended period of time, a charity will very quickly find itself on the same downward slope if it acquires such a score.

Organizational Capacity

This is not a widely held area in which to evaluate a charity. In fact, some in the industry are of the opinion that if a charity retains too high of an asset reserve it should be penalized. To some extent they have a point, but the reality is that in these times it is vital that charities be assured of their continued survival and ability to support their mission, even in the most difficult circumstances, which events have shown might last for a period of several years.

Building organizational capacity should be an integral

part of the normal operation and evolution of a charity. In the first years of this decade nearly 50% of charities increased their primary revenue by at least 7%. More than 40% of charities had at least one year's worth of working assets on which they could rely during a difficult period.

What should be examined is a charity's ability to support its services and programs over a period of time even in the face of adversity. In our view this is a plus, since it demonstrates to donors and potential donors that the charity will continue to grow and that it will maintain a level of financial stability that allows it to contribute to its mission. It is desirable that a charity plan for the long term and not allow its resources to become so diminished that it must devote time and effort to short-term fundraising to meet predictable financial demands.

Like all living organisms, charities must grow to survive and serve the needs of those to whom they give. The important aspect is the kind of growth that occurs. Primarily, growth for a charity means an ever-increasing stream of donations from a wide range of sources. This can include contributions by individuals, bequests, as well as donations from corporations, foundations and the government. It also includes membership dues, program revenue of various types, as well as fees and contracts. A charity should, at the minimum, expect to consistently outpace inflation in revenue growth. If it doesn't, it will find itself in very serious trouble.

As there is an increase in revenue growth, a charity should have a balanced growth in the programs and services it supports. If a charity is narrowly focused on one mission, it is reasonable to expect the efforts it supports for that mission to constantly expand. If a charity has a broader focus then it will routinely be addressing the needs of a greater constituency. In either case, the well-balanced charity will continue to support the increasing needs of society. Further, if a nonprofit takes the steps to gain greater efficiency and is *seen* by the public as being efficient, donors will be more inclined to support the nonprofit and its mission.

Adequate working capital is important to all charities as they rely on their reserves to survive difficult times. These can include a poorly performing economy or disasters which tend to draw a great volume of donations from their usual donor pool. Such was the case in the aftermath of 9/11. Lacking an adequate reserve often means letting valuable staff go, dropping important programs, acquiring debt, merging with another charity or even dissolving altogether.

But those charities with an adequate reserve do not face such difficult decisions. In fact, by working at building organizational capacity annually, in part through an increase in working capital, they will have a greater ability to enhance existing programs and add new ones.

How long a charity can sustain its current programs absent new revenue is a factor of its capital reserve. A ratio is calculated to rate a charity and allow its comparison in this area with other charities. One method used to evaluate a charity's working capital ratio is to divide its working capital by total expenses, including its distributions to existing services and programs, for the last fiscal year. For example, if a charity has $4.5 million in reserve and its total expenses for the most recent fiscal year were $2.8 million, it has a working capital ratio of 1.6 years. This ratio is then compared to peer charities.

Overall Scores and Ratings

Once ratings are established in the categories that encompass organizational efficiency and capacity, rating organizations such as the Charity Navigator then combine and convert them into a raw score on a scale between 0 and 10. This is in conjunction with assigning a star rating. A charity with a 10 score on the scale in a certain category would receive four stars. From this system comes a score for organizational efficiency, as well as one for organizational capacity.

Finally, a grand score which represents a charity's state

of affairs is calculated, and the charity is given an overall rating and a star score. Most donors who take the time to learn a certain charity's rating never go beyond these two scores.

Scoring Adjustments

While some charities are quite similar, it is not possible to force all of them into the same mold. Every charity to one degree or another has its own unique DNA. Identical management practices and charitable impulses can produce very different scores for certain charities. Some charitable causes, for example, lend themselves to a certain kind of fundraising which can affect fundraising costs positively or negatively. Some charities of necessity must have a presence in certain high-rent districts, while others can successfully operate from an obscure office on a back street.

Food banks, as an example, essentially exist as a hand-to-mouth operation given the nature of their largely perishable commodities and constant demand. They can be successful, and well managed, with very little capital reserve.

A community foundation in the same city would likely be a very different matter. Such foundations typically hold reserves which can sustain them for several years. Of necessity, these two types of charities must be considered in a different light because their raw scores could present a false picture of the reality. Adjustments are required in their scores so they can be properly rated.

In addition, some charities receive more donated services and goods. These can be difficult to place a value on, and how that value is determined can distort the numbers when attempting to establish a charity's efficiency.

Also, telephone calls and direct mailings can be intended to accomplish more than mere fundraising. They can, and often are, part of a broader education campaign. Just as a pollster might contact you not so much to learn where you stand on issues, but to inform or influence you about the issues, so it can be for charities.

It can be difficult to place a dollar figure on such efforts. How the expenses for these contacts are calculated and into what category they are placed can alter the numbers and ratio considerably. It is important to understand the potential and to know what formula has been applied in a specific case.

For this reason, and others, charities are not ranked. It just simply isn't a practical option and can be very misleading. Charities can be compared, one to another, or within a peer group, but a few minutes should be taken to examine scores in various categories and to understand what went into establishing the rating.

Ratios and Numbers

There are other areas explored in rating nonprofits. These are usually reduced to ratios which permit their ready comparison to other peer nonprofits. These are:

1. *Operating Ratio.* The most commonly used ratio, also known as the Current Ratio. It reflects how well a nonprofit can meet its short-term debt obligations, that is, short-term liquidity. The ratio is determined by dividing total assets by total liabilities. An Operating Ratio of one or greater is considered desirable.

2. *Debt/Equity Ratio.* This is the most commonly used measure of long-term liquidity. Long-term debt is divided by total net assets to arrive at the ratio. A better measure excludes assets that are permanently restricted for one reason or another.

3. *Financial Flexibility Ratios.* The flexibility here is the structure of the portfolio and how it is managed. Fixed assets, such as buildings, are considered to be less flexible than stocks, as an example. The ratio is calculated by taking fixed assets and dividing them by total assets. A score close to one indicates less flexibility.

4. *Net Income Ratio.* Nonprofits ideally zero out at the end of the fiscal year. If they have significant sums on hand

which are not immediately redirected to programs, then it reflects poorly on management and the nonprofit's commitment to its programs.

These ratios are a useful supplement to the others. Ratio analysis is its own specialized field and, properly conducted, can provide very valuable information when comparing one charity to another.

A function of the Molecular Consultant is to assist the nonprofit in sharing sufficient data with potential donors to appear sufficiently transparent. A charity's image is vital and most managers understand that, but potential donors must not struggle to understand your finances. A charity must not only conduct itself with propriety and financial efficiency, it must be seen to do so.

4.
FUNDRAISING

Fundraising is the lifeblood of any charity or nonprofit.

In a recent poll, 46% of charities reported that finding enough money was the single greatest challenge they faced, day in and day out. Keeping your doors open so that you can fulfill your mission is the constant concern and preoccupation of most charities, boards and staffs.

The situation is especially acute at the highest levels when it comes to unrestricted contributions, for there is an increasing tendency by substantial modern donors to specify the use to which their contribution is to be put. Simply obtaining the annual general operating money a charity requires can be daunting.

The Donor Pool

A certain flow of income is required for any nonprofit to remain viable and fulfill its mission. It is fundraising that is responsible for causing the income flow, and ideally it should be reasonably regular and predictable. When fundraising lags, so too does income; when fundraising is a success, the nonprofit will benefit enormously.

To maintain and enhance the integrity and credibility of

any nonprofit, it is vital that fundraising efforts be conducted in a manner that does not alienate donors and potential donors. Too often this is not the case. The media highlights the few nonprofits engaged in abusive fundraising practices thereby tainting the vast majority who adhere to sound fundraising practices. Because of adverse sensationalized publicity and poor reporting practices, charities are under ever-growing and intense scrutiny, and there is a movement afoot to impose even greater controls and regulations on them. This effort is being countered by an industry-wide effort at self-reform.

In most nonprofits, fundraising is practiced by tradition. The development director, the individual responsible for fundraising, will have a template of regular fundraising efforts and events that occur at specified times. The nonprofit, for example, might hold an annual holiday drive. It might conduct a letter or telephone solicitation, or both. Perhaps there is an annual fundraising dinner featuring entertainment, a raffle, a blind auction and other such activities. It is not uncommon for a nonprofit to receive the greatest part of its income flow from a single annual event.

Most nonprofits also have a portion of their donor pool who gives on a regular basis. They might receive a newsletter or other printed material to show them where their money is going and to keep them engaged with the nonprofit's mission. Some nonprofits even use television ads to raise money, though these are very much in the minority. Such ads are costly and require a designated staff to keep them airing at the appropriate times and locations.

The established donor pool is relied upon to produce an expected level of contributions and if, over the years, the amount begins to decline with the death of key donors that is only to be expected. This is a situation with which far too many nonprofits are faced. That is why most successful nonprofits have established planned giving and endowment programs to encourage their largest donors to establish endowments to perpetuate their gifts beyond their lifetime.

Not typically considered part of the fundraising team is the investment consultant. We consider that to be a waste of what could potentially be an extremely helpful resource. However, if an investment consultant is only going to invest your money, how does he or she add to the greater value of the nonprofit? A consultant, expert not only in capital markets, but also in the overall needs of a charity, that is, the Molecular Consultant, contributes so much more. He not only works to effectively manage the investment portfolio, in effect, raising money from the marketplace, but also helps in any number of ways, such as in isolating and identifying potential donors.

In our view, this is simply the natural extension of the investment consultant's role in the 21st century. The Molecular Consultant will possess a wide range of experience with a large number of endowments, charities and nonprofits. He will take an active part in your fundraising and will also have completed a demographic analysis of your potential donor pool. This provides him with a wealth of information on which he can draw to expand your declining pool of donors.

Growing the Pool

The demographic analysis of your potential donor pool, performed by a Molecular Consultant, will also include satellite fundraising evaluations. This is the means by which he will identify future donors who could have an interest in the mission of the nonprofit, but for any one of many reasons, do not give.

We refer to this as funneling. There are a certain number of people aware of your cause and a certain number of them willing to give. But because of those who drop out or pass on, you must continue funneling new people into your donor pool. The reality is that if you don't replenish donors, you will find it increasingly difficult to raise money.

Most development directors think of their donor pool as

a circle, but pools come in all shapes. The Molecular Consultant, for example, sees it in the shape of an egg. Those in the narrow part of the egg have yet to enter the circle that forms the active donor pool. What we do is take the information from the demographic analyses and utilize it to identify new people the development director would typically not approach. We then slowly seek to push that end of the egg down into the circle from which he draws contributions.

This is very useful for the typical development director who has a limited amount of time and will devote it to actually raising money. We compare him to a farmer harvesting while the Molecular Consultant is out there planting the seeds.

A common complaint of most charities is that there are already too many nonprofits competing for the available money. It is just one more act of cannibalism when a consultant holds a fundraiser and uses the same donor pool the development director employs. You want to go to people who've never given money to your nonprofit previously.

Now our fundraisers might not raise as much money initially because they are directed at embryonic contributors. The exposure is almost like an introduction to the nonprofit; the idea is to draw them closer. You're planting the seeds so that in time the development director can harvest them within his donor pool.

Employing all the Tools

Molecular Consultants strongly urge that nonprofits explore every available fundraising tool that would be applicable to their circumstances. Surprisingly, many do not consider tools that might work very well for them. There are a great number of vehicles donors and potential donors can use to transfer money and assets to a nonprofit of their choice. If a specific nonprofit isn't equipped, or experienced, with some of these vehicles they stand to lose a substantial contribution that will go to a similar charity that is so equipped. Not every tool works with every nonprofit, but they should all be considered.

These tools can offer significant donor tax advantages today for assets that don't actually transfer until later, and because of this are highly desirable. They include charitable gift annuities, life insurance, IRAs, grants through donor-advised funds, charitable remainder trusts, pooled income funds charitable lead trusts and even family foundations to coordinate family giving.

Too often we find charities that have two or three of the tools in place, but very rarely all of them. This is a serious error as it eliminates many giving tools proven effective in attracting substantial contributions. From our experience, many nonprofits do not even have in place a fully developed planned giving component. They tend to focus on raising immediate hard dollars. This is understandable given the constant need for administrative funds, but in focusing on dollars they neglect a wide range of giving tools.

The Molecular Consultant works with the development director to assure that every avenue is open to the charity to assist in raising money.

Integrity and Credibility

Though there exist in America approximately one million charities and nonprofits, public awareness of them was never keener than in the wake of the 2004 tsunami in South Asia. Customary appeals over the television, by mail or telephone solicitation that could be ignored were replaced by the vivid images of destruction and death. Americans were motivated to reach deeply into their pockets.

One consequence of that generosity was to subject long-existing nonprofits to heightened scrutiny. As Americans decided to give, they wanted to know that their contributions would go to making a difference and not to support administrative overhead. An example of this had taken place in

2001 when it was revealed that the American Red Cross was hoarding and/or misdirecting the $850 million given by millions for 9/11 relief and that large sums had been spent on non-9/11 activities. Public disclosure led to a reversal of the practice, but it served as a warning that some charities are not above exploiting a disaster.

Experts have analyzed the current state of affairs and concluded that to maintain public support, charities and nonprofits must:

1. **Be Transparent.** Donors and those seeking to donate must be able to readily learn about the charity to which they want to give. An open and informative – less common than you might think – website is the most efficient means for accomplishing this.

2. **Show Results.** It cannot be said too often, but today's donors want to know they are making a difference. They are willing to give large sums to specific charities, but only if they can see that the nonprofit is actually doing something positive with their money.

3. **Do What You Do Best.** In the tsunami tragedy several major charities were not well positioned to provide immediate relief while other organizations already had staff and resources on the ground. One such charity, the Natural Resources Defense Council, elected to direct donors to those charities and did not collect contributions itself. It passed on what could have been a very productive fundraising opportunity to maintain and enhance its public reputation.

4. **Don't Harass Donors.** The most common complaints about any charity or nonprofit are repeated mail and telephone solicitations. Not only can they irritate your donor pool they can drive donors away, and often do. Commercial telemarketers have developed such a bad reputation it is now recommended that charities and nonprofits stop general soliciting by telephone altogether. In addition, the type and frequency of mailings should be carefully reviewed.

The fundraising conduct of nonprofits can serve to improve their image and educate the giving public, or it can do the opposite. Shortsighted and abusive techniques can work for a single fundraising campaign or season, but in the end are detrimental to the nonprofit's mission.

A segment of the American population has already been permanently driven away from charities by past abuses; there's no reason to increase the number. Earn the trust of those in your donor pool and you will be rewarded.

Recommended Reforms

Integrity and credibility are essential for the long-term success of any nonprofit and charity. Unfortunately, scandals will always occur and it is essential that organizations inoculate themselves by taking certain obvious steps as recommended by Charity Navigator and others. When it comes to fundraising solicitations, they make three recommendations:

1. *Professional fundraisers should immediately identify who they work for and how much they take from each donation in any telephone solicitation.*

Though there is no limit placed on how much a charity pays to a professional fundraiser, the public has the right to know, especially if they are the target of a solicitation. Telemarketers typically receive 25 to 95 cents of every dollar they raise. Such practices are ultimately self-defeating, but they remain quite common. Donors are routinely misled into thinking their contribution will go to a worthy cause when much, even most, of it will go to the telemarketer. Telemarketer solicitations are one of the most objectionable fundraising techniques, yet charities in general refuse to condemn them, arguing they are simply business as usual.

2. *Mailing lists should not be shared without the expressed consent of the donor.*

Solicitation by mail is another form of fundraising subject to great criticism. Because of the way such letters are presented, many donors, especially the elderly, feel compelled to open every solicitation. Often they are angry that their original spontaneous act of charity in making a contribution has now made them the target to endless mail appeals, the cost of which to them often seems greater than the sum they gave. Worse, once they make a contribution, other charities begin flooding them with mail, clearly the result of the first charity sharing its mailing list. Though some charities allow donors to "opt out" of having their address made available, this option is not made prominent, or the donor is required to separately contact the charity for that purpose. Charities deserving of trust should not share their mailing lists, should restrict the number of solicitations they send a donor, and should make it simple for a donor to decline receiving future solicitations.

3. *Every fundraising appeal should contain the nonprofit's tax identification number, a valid telephone contact number and the address on their IRS form 990.*

Donors are often confused about the various charities that approach them. These charities use different names, have addresses in various states, and have no reply information except a P. O. Box. Charities should provide the basic information above and not seek to confuse donors into making additional contributions.

Though fundraising abuses are the most conspicuous, there are other related issues such as governance and accountability. For them, Charity Navigator has three recommendations:

1. *All board members should serve without compensation, except for the Chief Executive who serves ex officio.*

Service on the board of directors of any charity or nonprofit should be voluntary. Any form of compensation adversely impacts the public perception of its integrity.

2. *All compensation that is provided to officers, directors, trustees and key employees from a charity and all of its*

501 [c] related organizations should be included on page 4 of the form 990.

It is, regrettably, very common for charity CEOs to be paid through multiple affiliated organizations, allowing the charity to present a false picture of the CEOs compensation. This information is typically spread out through the various 990s and is not easily identified. All sums paid, including consulting fees, should be listed in a single location.

3. *When a program expense is identified as "education," the nonprofit should indicate whether or not the materials were bundled with a fundraising appeal.*

Disguising fundraising appeals as educational materials is another unfortunate practice in which too many nonprofits engage. One well-known health research charity, for example, incurs 25% of its education costs in conjunction with its fundraising appeals. If this is a legitimate way to label expenses, nonprofits should simply disclose it to the public.

The common theme in all of these recommendations is to bring about changes that will enhance the integrity and credibility of nonprofits and charities in their fundraising efforts. It should be understood that while the abuses noted can be effective in the short-run, over time they harm the nonprofit and adversely impact the nonprofit sector. Abusive or misleading practices should have no place in the fund-raising of any legitimate nonprofit.

There is an important reason for the charitable sector to police itself. Donors have told Congress that they are fed up with nonprofits that persist in engaging in abusive practices. Congress has conducted hearings into the conduct of nonprofits and is increasingly moving towards enforcing reform by statute. This is nearly always undesirable since it harms the reputation of charities in the public eye, mandates a "one size fits all" solution to perceived problems, and increases government regulation over, and interference with, charities and nonprofits. One unfortunate result will be that more donor money than ever must be spent on lawyers, accountants and staff to comply with new regulations.

Key recommendation from Senate hearings have included:

- Adoption of conflict-of-interest policies.
- Organizations with $2 million or more in revenue being required to have an outside audit.
- Increasing the budget for the Internal Revenue Service to enforce existing laws.

Surely it is better that the solutions to the persistent abuses of a small minority of nonprofits should come from voluntary actions and compliance with guidelines.

Under very active consideration is a change in federal law mandating that all nonprofits and charities undergo a government review of their status every five years. The resources an organization would be compelled to commit to such a review would be extraordinary, as the legal standing of the organization would be at stake, and the reviews would serve to bleed even more funds from its mission.

Gifts Other Than in Cash

We've all seen the television commercials urging you to give your unneeded car to charity. That is just one example of a gift other than cash. Though such write-offs are rarely the primary reason for the donation, they do make it easier to solicit and receive such gifts.

Every day, in every charity dining room in America, volunteers give their time to cook meals, ladle out food and clean up. In addition, donors give professional services such as accounting or legal help; surplus products such as computers, land and buildings; and other non-cash gifts. In many cases these contributions cannot be deducted from their taxes, yet people continue to give.

There have been, and are, many abuses in this system, so not surprisingly Congress is eyeing this area very closely.

Many lawmakers hold the view that the deductions now permitted for such donations are excessive and are considering reducing, or even eliminating them. The financial allure to Congress is very strong as it is estimated that the federal government could receive an additional $2.5 billion in less than a decade with such an alteration in the law.

Governance

The focus of proposed changes to nonprofit governance are meant to prevent individuals from gaining improper financial advantage through charitable work, improve oversight of fiscal conduct, and to create greater organizational transparency for donors, potential donors and the public in general.

There is also an ongoing concern over the conduct of some charities and nonprofits that participate in suspect, or even illegal, tax shelters. Here the focus has been on the accountants and others who omit key information or engage in misrepresenting the facts when they prepare tax returns and disclosure forms. To solve this problem, it is proposed that greater emphasis be placed on criminal prosecutions.

Several nonprofit and charitable organizations in a coalition are spearheading efforts for such changes to occur voluntarily and without government action.

Disclosure and Enforcement

To this end, the nonprofit coalition spearheaded by Independent Sector, a nonpartisan coalition of approximately 500 nonprofit organizations, is advocating certain measures all charities and nonprofits should embrace. It is also encouraging increased fines against wrongdoers and supports changes in the law which make that more likely.

These recommended measures include ensuring that tax returns are signed by the chief executive officer, as is the case in public companies as mandated by the Sarbanes-Oxley Act. In addition, charities and nonprofits should have an outside audit if their annual revenue is $2 million or more. They should also retain an outside public accountant to review their finances if their annual revenue is greater than half a million dollars, but less than $2 million.

The coalition advocates that the Internal Revenue Service require all nonprofits to report if they have a conflict-of-interest policy. Such conflicts are too common and have resulted in abuses. They recommend the tax-exempt status of such nonprofits be suspended if they do not make such a disclosure for two consecutive years and that penalties against them be rigorously enforced.

When it comes to governance, the coalition advocates that charities and nonprofits adopt and enforce a conflict-of-interest policy. It also advocates that they include individuals on their boards who possess financial literacy. They urge that organizations establish a separate board committee assigned to oversee audits. In addition, policies should be in place to encourage whistleblowers to report violations of procedures or of the law.

Change is coming, both in fundraising activities and in how nonprofits conduct their affairs. Whether it will be the result of voluntary steps taken by the nonprofit industry, the consequence of new laws and enforcement practices, or a combination of both, remains uncertain. What is certain is that the need for boards and managers to have available a consultant with broad knowledge of these issues has never been more vital.

5.
FIDUCIARY RESPONSIBILITY

Nonprofits have a fundamental obligation to conduct their affairs, financial and otherwise, in a responsible and transparent manner. It's not only sound practice; it is intrinsic to the long-term vitality and success of the organization, especially during this time when the modern donor is making ever-greater contributions.

The Fiduciary

In general, a fiduciary is anyone who acts for the benefit of another; in which the beneficiary relies on the fiduciary with trust and in which the fiduciary must behave with good faith, keeping uppermost in mind the best interests of the beneficiary.

An investment fiduciary is someone who manages property or assets for the benefit of another, or who exercises discretionary control of such assets, or a professional placed in a position of trust, providing comprehensive and continuing investment advice.

Traditionally those considered to be fiduciaries include attorneys, accountants, executors, money managers, trustees of private trusts, investment consultants, and committee members for foundations, endowments and retirement plans. Broken into its component parts, a fiduciary is any person who:

- Exercises discretionary control over management, or the management and disposition, of assets.
- Provides investment advice for a fee or other compensation, or has the authority to do so.
- Has discretionary authority over the organization's administration, whether it is exercised or not.

Because of the very nature of the trust, the duties imposed on a fiduciary are significant, with legal ramifications if not properly exercised. Fiduciary status always remains with the fiduciary and cannot be delegated away to another or a third party, though there is a reduced liability through the use of a qualified consultant. The fiduciary capacity is established not from a title, but through the actions and responsibilities imposed by the functions of the position.

There is a common misconception that outsourcing administration or consultation to others means transferring the fiduciary responsibility. Except as mentioned, that is not the case. It is also often thought that providing staff with investment options and allowing them to make decisions from those options relieves the obligation of the fiduciary. That also is not the case. It is simply not possible for the fiduciary to be inoculated through such actions, as they are deemed to demonstrate a lack of prudence.

The execution of fiduciary duty is also not in simply making good investment decisions or in selecting competent managers. It is required that the fiduciary have in place a proper process for making those decisions. In fact, the fiduciary responsibility can be said to be inherently based on process. It is anticipated that from a properly prepared and applied process comes untainted decision-making.

In fulfilling their duties, fiduciaries must possess a reasonable understanding of the available investment alternatives, as well as the complete variety of choices. In addition, proper and detailed records must be maintained which fully disclose the process and how the eventual decision was reached.

Duties of the Fiduciary

A fiduciary must strictly adhere to the mission of the nonprofit. This may seem obvious, but it is crucial to proper conduct. The primary obligation of a fiduciary is to manage the portfolio assets in the interests of the participants and beneficiaries. He or she is required to follow the terms of the adopted Investment Policy Statement, which is the formal statement of the nonprofit's investment strategy. Since a fiduciary must exercise his or her decision-making in the best interest of the beneficiary, faced with two investments of equal security, he or she is obligated to take the one with the greater prospect of return.

The fiduciary must also act in the *sole* interest of the beneficiary. No other considerations, no matter how important or praiseworthy, may affect it.

A fiduciary also has an obligation to perform his or her duties in a certain prescribed manner. The expectations are not complicated and are often self-evident. A fiduciary must exercise the utmost care to acquire sufficient information to ensure the maximum protection of the assets. He or she must honestly provide full disclosure of all material facts which could in any way influence the decision-making process.

In addition, the fiduciary must demonstrate loyalty to the nonprofit, in part by refraining from acquiring an adverse interest, but also by providing full disclosure and by not personally profiting from the position. All these functions must be performed in good faith, truthfully, honestly, with integrity, and with moral principles and sound character.

In simpler times, the fiduciary responsibility of a board member or manager to any charity or nonprofit was a relatively straightforward matter. What was asked was that he or she conduct themselves as a "prudent man." Nonprofits are now such a significant force in our nation's economy, and investment vehicles have become so diverse, that far more is required. Today's board members and managers face new and unprecedented concerns.

Current Issues

Nonprofits generally hold resources far greater than they have ever possessed in the past. The sums can be enormous and a bit overwhelming, especially to a traditional administration. Not surprisingly, properly and efficiently managing such a portfolio is often a challenge, and beyond the scope and experience of existing staff.

In the boom years of the 1990s, when much of this value was created, this was not a significant issue, since most responsible investments delivered a high rate of return, but with the meltdown of the stock market many nonprofits have found themselves in very difficult financial straits. Managing resources in such a problematic environment has proven beyond the abilities of large numbers of boards and managers, with adverse consequences for their organizations.

One of the lessons taken from the experiences of the last decade has been a heightened sense of risk aversion. The unprecedented growth in the value of assets in the 1990s, followed by an equally unprecedented drop in value and rate of return, has caused, in many cases, an unwillingness to engage in adequately aggressive investment out of fear of new losses and blame.

Though inflation has been at modern record lows during this time, given the overriding economic realities it cannot be expected to remain so docile indefinitely. Charities and nonprofits must be prepared for a resurgence of this asset-devouring specter. Funds too heavily invested in fixed-income vehicles can be potentially devastated by the resurgence of inflation. The targeted giving rate, 5% in most cases, can cut negatively into a portfolio in such circumstances.

Balancing future anticipated donations against future giving has never been more challenging. Being too conservative in approach can be as problematic as being too aggressive. The steady rise in investment income, along with a predictable donor pattern, adjusted to giving needs, is now a phenomenon of the past. Never before has the immediate future appeared so uncertain, even as the prospects are so rosy for the coming decades.

Volatility in the market always exists no matter how an endowment seeks to avoid it. It is no less a force today than ever before, and probably a greater one, with all the risk that accompanies it. The war on terror can be expected to last at least a decade, and during that time our financial institutions will remain targets of physical and infrastructure attacks. While we can hope another devastating attack will not be successful, we cannot rule out the possibility. It serves to add another layer of volatility to investment decision-making.

The role of government and politics must also be taken into account. Nonprofits have always been responsive to political forces, never more so than today. Laws govern much of how they operate and they possess significant assets which can affect public policy, so it is unavoidable. Recent scandals in certain philanthropies, as well as those on Wall Street, have only heightened regulatory interest. The Patriot Act and the use of certain charities to direct money to terrorists has placed all charities and nonprofits under the microscope, and it isn't going to get any better. Where donations come from and where the money is given has never before received such attention. In fact, another tragic event will certainly cause even greater scrutiny than we now face.

While currently intended just for publicly held companies, the standards and expectations of the Sarbanes-Oxley Act are quickly becoming universal and are rapidly extending into charities and nonprofits. The governance of board members and managers, as well as their salaries, expenses and administrative overhead, are all, and will continue to be, areas of close examination.

Fewer and fewer boards and managers are attempting to deal with the myriad burgeoning issues on their own. The traditional investment consultant is normally focused on investment issues and rarely considers such matters. The nonprofit which continues with "business as usual" is headed for serious difficulties, and the consequences for individual board members and managers can be disastrous. There has never been a time of greater need for qualified professional assistance in the form of the Molecular Consultant.

Growing Fiduciary Responsibilities

The traditional definition of the fiduciary as someone who acts in a position of trust for the benefit of, or on behalf of, another has been steadily expanded in recent years, primarily by the courts, to also include anyone exercising discretionary control over fund management or the dispersal and/or management of assets. The definition today includes compensated independent consultants rendering investment advice concerning those assets.

In modern investment management, decisions should be made in the context of the total portfolio; that is, diversify assets to guard against potential large declines in value. To this end, generally accepted fiduciary conduct includes a number of obligations. The fiduciary must follow or prepare a written Investment Policy Statement and document the process used to arrive at investment decisions. The fiduciary must diversify portfolio assets, taking into honest consideration specific risk/return objectives of the beneficiaries. He or she should highly consider also employing the services of professional money managers ['prudent experts'] in arriving at investment decisions.

In addition, the fiduciary must also control and account for, or oversee, the controlling and accounting for all investment expenses, and monitor the activities of all organization money managers and service providers. And finally, the fiduciary must avoid every conflict of interest, and is wise to avoid even the appearance of one.

Training, education and experience in each of these are essential to any board, board member or nonprofit manager.

The Prudent Investor

There is much harm the imprudent or dishonest fiduciary or investment consultant can cause or allow to happen. They can participate in speculative investments without proper research and information-gathering. They can engage in excessive trading [known as 'churning'] to produce transaction fees. They can engage in short-term trading of mutual funds to the same end, or establish phony accounts with which to conduct business otherwise prohibited. They can make unauthorized transactions or misuse funds. They can even engage in fraud, forgery, or the misstatement or deletion of key information. For good reason, standards of conduct and expectations of behavior for the fiduciary have long been established.

Until the 1950s, the primary principle which governed the conduct of a fiduciary was called the "Prudent Man Rule." The phrase comes from an 1830 court decision in *Harvard v. Amory* in which Judge Samuel Putman addressed the issue that risk must be considered along with return, and wrote:

Do what you will, the capital is at hazard. All that can be required of a trustee to invest is that he shall conduct himself faithfully and exercise a sound discretion. He is to observe how men of prudence, discretion, and intelligence managed their own affairs, considering the probable income, as well as the probable safety of the capital to be invested.

In practice this came to mean that a fiduciary need only behave towards those funds entrusted to him or her in a prudent manner. Over the coming century it was apparent that there were a number of holes in this approach when it came to application because the Prudent Man Rule was a generalized standard that lacked a specific definition. In particular, it failed to address evolving potential conflicts of interest and the application of investments.

Then in the 1950s, Dr. Harry Markowitz called into question a number of assumptions about sound investment policy for organizations. He eventually earned a Nobel Prize in economics for his work, and from it came the "Prudent Investor Rule." It has been summarized in this way: "Investments shall be made with judgment and care, under circumstances then prevailing, which persons of prudence, discretion and intelligence exercise in the management of their own affairs, not for speculation, but for investment, considering the probable safety of their capital as well as the probable income to be derived."

The Prudent Investor Rule requires trustees to emphasize total return, not just preservation of capital. This had the affect of profoundly altering the responsibilities of fiduciaries and changed the nature of investments for nonprofits. There are today five steps in the recognized prudent process:

1. *Analyze Your Current Position.* Carefully consider the mission of the organization as well as the nature of the investment portfolio. These include brokerage relationships, accounting assumptions, legal issues and formalized policies, to name a few. You should also thoroughly analyze your spending policy, using any of several accepted useful tools.

2. *Create an Optimal Portfolio.* Diversification is fundamental to managing risk. For this reason, asset allocation decisions are crucial. In any potential investment there are trade-offs between return and risk. They are the key to sound investment. An optimized portfolio will have managed risk within a commonly accepted range and in compliance with a nonprofit's established Investment Policy Statement.

3. *Formalize the Investment Policy.* The investment policy

of a charity or nonprofit must not only follow the standards of the Prudent Investor, but it must be set down in writing. This serves as a guide to the fiduciary, ensures continuity in objectives, provides standards, and allows new trustees and managers to participate effectively in a shorter timeframe. It must include investment guidelines, allocation standards, and investment objectives, and set the standard for selecting investment managers.

4. ***Implementing the Written Policy.*** Understand that though trustees and managers will come from a variety of backgrounds and bring to a nonprofit a great deal of experience, they are held to the same level of expertise as a professional investment consultant. It is necessary that qualified professionals be included in turning the Investment Policy Statement into actual investments. Investment funds and managers must meet rigorous standards. Investment managers must also be a good "fit" for the goals of the fiduciaries.

5. ***Regular Review.*** Monitoring investment performance is as important as the other four steps. Performance should be regularly evaluated. The performance of investment managers should be compared to that of their peers and similar portfolios. Such regular review will allow fiduciaries to evaluate performance and will assist them in decision-making. It will also provide an opportunity for discussion by the board members and/or managers concerning possible changes or difficulties that might exist.

It is anticipated that both the legal and practical scrutiny of a fiduciary will continue to increase in the future. Such examination will be intense and come from many sources for any number of reasons. It is estimated that both formal complaints and lawsuits alleging misconduct against fiduciaries will become more and more common. Given history, some of these allegations will certainly be true, but most of them can be avoided with a proper understanding of fiduciary responsibilities and with proper education and training.

In the final analysis, fiduciary liability is not the result of the performance of the portfolio, but rather whether or not sound investment practices and processes have been adhered to.

Effective Use of Professional Consultants

It is no longer expected that a fiduciary necessarily possess the wide range of specialized knowledge needed to make informed investment decisions. The investment world has simply become too complicated. But it is expected that in designating investment management specialists, due diligence will be exercised in the process and it is understood that the fiduciary still has an obligatory role in all investment decision-making. For this reason, the proper selection and supervision of professional consultants is vital.

Investment management consulting is an emerging profession, so care must be exercised in making such a selection. Given the heightened level of scrutiny nonprofits now face, the potential adverse consequences for fiduciaries, and the often complex nature of investing and maintaining a large portfolio, such experts have never been more valuable. They can unburden a board and managers from the persistent details that inevitably accompany investment decisions and direct them into sound investment vehicles.

The initial part of the selection process is to find an investment consultant with whom you are comfortable and one who effectively communicates ideas and concepts to you. If you find a personality to be annoying, cloying or oppressive, you will not establish and maintain the kind of essential relationship your obligations and common sense dictate. Unfortunately, for too many boards the process stops here. Remember: an expensive suit and winning manner by themselves mean almost nothing and are available to anyone trying to sell a bill of goods.

Keep in mind that financial and investment concepts can be presented in an overly complex, jargon-filled manner that is off-putting and needlessly confusing. These concepts are not great mysteries and can be articulated in down-to-earth simple language and writing. For all the new financial vehicles and the myriad names given to them, basic sound investing principles are essentially unchanged. Find a consultant who can relate them in a way you understand and who has a personality and manner you find agreeable for the job.

Investment consultants can be affiliated with a large financial services company, one that is a household name, or they can be independent. The most important step in identifying an investment consultant is to determine their qualifications and experience. Certain professional designations such as Certified Investment Management Consultant [CIMC], Certified Investment Management Analyst [CIMA], or the equivalent, can be very helpful. You should know the number of years of specialized experience the consultant has. His or her areas of expertise should include:

- Modern investment theory
- Investment policy development
- Investment management
- Manager selection, and
- Performance monitoring

These are all areas which are of concern to you, and the greater the experience and knowledge your potential investment consultant has, the more likely it will be that he or she will perform ably.

It is also important to receive meaningful referrals from other investors with whom the consultant has done business. Be certain to fully understand the nature of the relationship and to weed out relatives, personal friends, or friends of friends doing someone a favor in making a recommendation. Ideally, you want to speak to members of similar boards and managers who have had a long association with your prospective investment consultant. Anyone seeking such a position with you should have no difficulty in directing you to satisfied customers. If what you receive instead is a good story, beware.

Also, keep in mind that the kind of consultant you seek does not sell products and is completely free of other potential conflicts of interest. And if you are aggressively, or even subtly, directed to a certain money manager, mutual fund or other specific product, look elsewhere and end your association.

Though it is not commonly listed as a qualification, you also want someone who cares about what you do. The ideal investment consultant will personally be involved on a voluntary basis in charities and giving. His or her roots will be deep and heartfelt. Such a consultant will bring to you a dimension and commitment no amount of money can buy.

For all this, and given the wide range of needs, retaining the services of an investment consultant with limited expertise and scope is foolhardy. A Molecular Consultant can provide you with a wide range of valuable advice and bring to the table experience that can be invaluable in many, many areas other than portfolio management.

Investor Resources

The best known and most highly respected organization of professional investment consultants working with non-profits is the Investment Management Consultants Association [IMCA]. It provides professional recognition, ongoing education, and information on the evolving industry, as well as services for its members. It is an invaluable resource for fiduciaries.

Though not restricted strictly to fiduciary responsibilities, one of the more useful locations for information of all kinds relating to charities is CharityNavigator.org. Founded in 2001, it has quickly established itself as a major source for information relating to American charities and should be regular viewing for any board member or manager.

There are a number of other reliable resources which can be consulted and will be known to most investment consultants.

Training and Education of Fiduciaries

Given the degree of their exposure, it is understandable that board members are now far more aggressive in scrutinizing their organizations. They recognize their responsibility for the nonprofit to be well-managed. Board members also understand the need for their nonprofit to withstand the spotlight of official and public disclosure should it ever be directed at them. They want to know what their personal fiduciary responsibility is, if for no other reason than to protect themselves.

For these, and other reasons, training and educating a board member on his or her duties is no longer considered desirable, but is viewed as essential. Any charity or nonprofit which fails to provide such training and education will find it increasingly difficult to attract new, qualified board members.

It is quite common, indeed typical, for a new fiduciary to have no idea what responsibilities are involved. This is still another reason why such training and continuing education is so vital. The Molecular Consultant will be prepared to provide that essential first period of training to any new board member. He will know what is important and see that you learn about it.

Such training and ongoing education are important functions of the Molecular Consultant. Because of Sarbanes-Oxley, the Patriot Act, and heightened interest by the Better Business Bureau, many of those considering serving today on boards are deciding to write a check instead. Charities and nonprofits simply are finding it increasingly difficult to locate responsible people to serve. The most able and qualified have always been difficult to recruit. Such training and education assures prospects that they can perform their duties and not be at risk.

Such an ongoing comprehensive program is good for any nonprofit because when it has an opening on its board it can show that it provides proper training and educational support to board members.

These are demanding times for charities and nonprofits, but they are also times of enormous opportunity. Providing for the legitimate concerns of those who function in a fiduciary capacity is a key step in favorably positioning your nonprofit for the years to come.

6.
ASSET ALLOCATION

Asset allocation is the process for determining how to divide a portfolio among different asset classes. It is the initial step towards achieving a nonprofit's investment goals. Theoreticians and practitioners agree that the asset allocation is typically the most important decision made by the investor as it is the most significant factor impacting the overall investment performance of a nonprofit.

The reason for this is that asset allocation allows you to examine the correlation between the various risk and return levels and is the method through which risk is reduced. The asset allocation is dependent on the nonprofit's identified investment program objectives and anticipated market behavior.

The Asset Allocation Analysis

While the actual asset allocation depends on the existing condition of the market, a portfolio's strategic asset allocation is the single most significant factor impacting the portfolio's overall performance. The greatest measure of return is the consequence of the asset classes selected and of the investment styles implemented, as well as the allocation of assets among the classes and styles.

Not only does asset allocation produce the greatest portion of a portfolio's return, it is also the most significant aspect of the investment process that is under the direct control of the board. The various money managers will nave discretionary control in selecting specific investment vehicles, but it is the board that designates the asset classes, investment styles and asset allocation. It is also the board that picks the money managers whose performance is compatible with those decisions and can implement them in actual practice, setting in place the investment policy agreed.

To provide the necessary information for the various decisions, the board will conduct an Asset Allocation Analysis, or AAA. This is typically considered to be the first step in implementing the portfolio's investment objectives and putting them into place. The investment program objectives will serve to define the nonprofit's goals. This analysis provides the framework for determining the placement of the portfolio to achieve those objectives.

The AAA is intended to produce the proper mix of asset classes and investment styles. The analysis will focus on the desired rate of return and the established risk tolerance. In other words, it will seek to identify the level of risk an individual account is likely to incur to reach a given rate of return. If the nonprofit desires to limit its risk exposure, the AAA will identify the gain that can be reasonably anticipated. The AAA will provide a broad range of asset allocation choices in addressing each of these issues.

As is the case in nearly all investment analysis, the guidance provided by the AAA is based on the assumptions and criteria that are selected. They relate to the various categories of the nonprofit's overall investment program as well as to the market's performance. They can, and usually will, vary considerably from nonprofit to nonprofit, even those generally considered to be within the same peer group. Every situation is unique.

Types of Risk in Asset Allocation

Risk and return go hand in hand. Risk, as it applies to life, is composed of exposure and uncertainty. In investments, risk can include any number of factors as well. One of the leading concepts concerning investment risk is standard deviation, which is simply the measure of the dispersion of a set of data from its average. The more spread the data, the higher the deviation. In finance, standard deviation is applied to the annual rate of return of an investment to measure the investment's volatility.

There is a wide range of risks associated with nonprofit investing. Every investment vehicle faces different types of risks and to varying degrees. Risks for an investment can range from something as obvious as timing to something as tedious and unexpected as liquidity.

The first type of risk is one that investors can control on an individual level. This includes both timing and tenure risks. Timing means when the investment is made. Tenure is the risk an investor faces by holding an investment over a certain timeframe. This includes a shift in markets over time while holding an asset, subjecting the investor to inflation changes, even the risk of a company going bankrupt.

The next group of risks are those associated with a company:

- Company financial risk is the risk that a company will be excessively financed by debt. In such a case, a company is burdened with debt, which in turn means less growth and value.
- Management risk is the risk that all companies face if they are poorly run. A company poorly managed will see drastic drops in stock prices, loss of dividend payments and an inability to grow.

Then there is market risk. This is the risk of the overall market not performing well, thus causing individual securities to suffer. The factors that affect market risk, among others, include liquidity, which is the risk that comes from losing value when selling an asset.

There is interest rate risk: that is, the risk that bonds will lose money when interest rates fluctuate, as they often do. Inflation risk is the risk associated with the inflation of the money you place into an investment. It can be worth less when you take it out of that investment because of rising inflation during the timeframe in which you held the investment. Exchange rate risk is the risk that the dollar might lose value in comparison to the currency of foreign countries.

This can severely harm investors with international assets. And finally, there is reinvestment risk: that is, the risk that comes when changing from one investment vehicle to another and losing money in the new investment because it did not perform as well as the old one.

The last common group of investment risk is national and international risk. These risks involve events and regulations which impact investment markets. The first of this type is the risk that a country's economy will not perform well, which can cause many problems for an investor, including job loss, a downturn in stock prices and many other factors which contribute to or are affected by national economy performance. There is also industry risk, which is the danger of a specific industry performing poorly.

Investors also face two more very tricky types of national risk, which are taxes and political risks. Tax risks are just that, the risk that taxes will diminish your profit as an investor. The more subtle downside of taxes is that a rise in taxes will frequently reduce the attractive nature of investing to many individuals, causing an overall drop in the markets.

Political risk is the danger of political changes such as prohibitive licensing or the election or placement of individuals into power who may be detrimental to an investment sector. These political risks can also include wars and trade embargoes.

The various types of risk which investors face come on many levels. Investment vehicles will be differently affected in each of them, which in turn means that as an investor you must deal with, or at least be aware of, them.

Risk and Portfolio Performance

Investors traditionally measured risk to maximize their returns by simply measuring the risk of individual investments. This meant that an investor would review a company, its past performance, its potential for growth and other factors in determining the potential risk versus reward for a single stock. They would then invest in those stocks that best measured up. While this could result in safe returns, the results were often unpredictably disastrous.

With the knowledge that risk is *inherent* in investing, economists and finance professionals set out to minimize the negative affects of risk on portfolio performance. Dr. Harry Markowitz published his theory in a 1952 *Journal of Finance* article entitled *Portfolio Selection.*

Markowitz's theory argued that the way to optimize the performance of a portfolio was not to analyze investments simply on a company-to-company basis. Rather, Markowitz suggested stepping back and looking at risk for an entire portfolio. Determining how to counteract risk by shifting exposure [by allocating assets] and understanding that uncertainty cannot be changed is largely what made this approach a success. Markowitz's Modern Portfolio Theory plays to the natural unpredictability of the financial market by using the mathematics of diversification. Rather than picking stocks based on risk versus return, it allocates and diversifies an entire portfolio based on an overall tolerance of risk versus reward based on an individual investor's needs and goals.

As part of his theories, Markowitz created what is known as the Efficient Frontier. This consists of a curve along a graph which compares risk and expected return at varying percentages of asset allocation. It is along this curve that any portfolio should be located in order to maximize return at any given level of risk. This was Markowitz's contribution to the financial world, and it is applied today in every prudent practice of asset allocation because it allows the identification of specific needs of an organization based on risk tolerances. Through that process an asset allocation is identified on the Efficient Frontier. The concept of the Efficient Frontier makes it possible for a nonprofit to diversify its investments in such a way as to optimize returns.

Markowitz understood that there is a very real, yet ephemeral, relationship between market volatility and return. In fact, risk is usually defined as a manifestation of market volatility, and in general, the greater the volatility, the greater the gain potential; the less the volatility, the lower the rate of return.

Even for the expert, defining risk can be elusive. Risk has many dimensions and must be analyzed from more than one perspective. These include the potentially adverse consequences of excessive market volatility, the maintenance of buying and spending power for the nonprofit, and the need to attain and sustain the rate of anticipated gain. This is all affected by the board's risk tolerance, and that tolerance is a direct manifestation of the tolerance of each member.

A retired executive or elderly widow will generally have a higher aversion to risk, while a businessman in his 30s would typically be more inclined to accept greater risk in making investment decisions. We are the reflection of our life experiences and expectations for the future. In most cases, though not all, the more years we have lived, the more conservative becomes our approach to investment decisions.

With a wide range of investment styles and a diverse selection of asset classes, the key factor for the board remains the level of risk tolerance. It is in this regard that the Asset Allocation Analysis plays such a vital role.

In general, there are two approaches to risk tolerance:

- The basic asset allocation adjustment approach encompasses only the risk/return dimension of a stock, bond and cash distribution. This is analyzed as aggressive, that is, with a greater percentage of stocks; moderate, with more balanced percentages; and conservative, that is, with a greater percentage placed in bonds.
- The style category adjustment approach relies primarily on the initial asset allocation and takes into consideration the timeframe and return expectations. From this the investment categories deemed to be most appropriate are selected. This approach tends to be more customized in implementing an investment strategy.

Through the category allocation approach the various levels of risk tolerance are combined with a wide variety of gain objectives and various timeframes. Different risk tolerances can be employed by adjusting the timeframe and return expectations in making the specific vehicle selection. There is a place for both short and long-term expectations and for conservative, moderate and aggressive management styles. Maintaining the proper balance assures that the risk tolerance is adhered to.

Risk tolerance is typically considered in light of the volatility in the various values of stocks and bonds. These two investment vehicles are carefully balanced in a portfolio and each carries with it its own risk and gain issues. Considering them by category they exhibit different properties which must be taken into account.

Establishing Risk Tolerance

Risk tolerance is a key component in devising the optimal investment strategy for a nonprofit and is a focus of the AAA. Taken along with the timeframe, portfolio size and return expectations, it is usually the single most significant issue. It is used to establish category allocations and to assist in determining specific investment vehicles. The essential prerequisite is to define all objectives and preferences in order to set in place the asset allocation strategy.

In considering any investment strategy or asset allocation the board must also consider what is called "probability distribution." This means taking into consideration every possible consequence and the related probabilities of each occurring. The probability distribution can be continuous, as when all potential outcomes constitute a continuous sweep.

In determining risk tolerance there are at least four considerations:

- Volatility is inherent in any investment so be honest in considering not just the potential gain, but also the potential loss.
- Be certain to establish your risk tolerance level before making any investment decision and assure that each investment conforms to it.
- Diversify the portfolio into an optimal spread of investment categories.
- Address risk tolerance and reestablish it no less than once a year. The market, even the nonprofit itself, will change, simply because change is inevitable.

Risk is an important factor in preparing the AAA, yet it is illusive. To identify risk, it is generally regarded from several perspectives. These include the possible impact of a decline in purchasing power, the potential in creating greater volatility and the need to achieve the anticipated gain. The AAA process will include a review of the various asset classes and different investment styles commonly accepted to assist in determining which are appropriate to actually include in the AAA in accordance with the nonprofit's established level of risk tolerance. Also to be considered is the nonprofit's actual experience in making investments

The Criteria

The preparation of the Asset Allocation Analysis is affected by three key factors that exist in every nonprofit's investment program. These are:

- The specified timeframe
- The desired rate of return
- The level of risk tolerance

While all three are important, the one that will have the greatest impact is the timeframe, also called the time horizon. In other words, how quickly the nonprofit wants a certain gain dictates the degree of risk to be assumed. From that comes the determination of the types of investments to be included in the portfolio. Most nonprofits are intended to function in perpetuity and it may seem at first glance that timeframe is not of consequence. But the reality is that even a long-term investment program is subject to the adverse effects of short-term volatility.

The desired rate of return is the consequence itself of three interrelated functions. These are:

- The anticipated rate of inflation.
- The nonprofit's spending policy.
- The desired rate of growth.

These three variables taken together comprise the total return objective. The greater the desired rate of return, the greater is the need for an extended timeframe and the acceptance of a more liberal risk tolerance. In this way, an asset allocation can be implemented with the capacity to generate the desired gain.

The AAA is a tool designed to assist the nonprofit in making the most appropriate asset allocation for their needs, within the parameters the board has established. It is not a precise process that can unerringly predict the future and guarantee a given rate of return. However, if properly used the AAA can greatly reduce risk and increase returns.

Establishing the Distribution Percentage

More from tradition than for any other reason, American nonprofits tend to follow a distribution of 60% stock, 30% bonds and 10% cash or its equivalent. While it is true that statutes and regulations influence this mix, a much stronger motivator comes from the fact that this is the distribution followed by most nonprofits. There is no financial or practical reason to consider such a distribution to be optimal. In Canada, for example, pension funds tend to have a mix of 40% stocks and 60% fixed income, while life insurance annuities are a strong component of European pension funds.

The reality faced by the vast majority of nonprofits is that the proper asset allocation for them can be significantly different from that of other nonprofits, even from those within their own peer group. Missions, investment objectives, portfolio size and other factors make an enormous difference, even for seemingly very similar nonprofits. This is but one reason that the AAA is such an essential step in helping to make specific investment decisions.

The Market Analysis

What must also be analyzed to achieve an appropriate asset allocation is the market itself along with a determination of the specific variables which will be employed in conducting the AAA. This begins by preparing a list of various asset classes and investment styles that are agreed will be considered as having a place in the adopted investment program. This is a four-step process:

1. *Allocation Parameters.* A well-balanced portfolio should not be skewed toward one style of investment or certain asset classes because of changes that occur from market conditions. To this end, it is important to establish the

maximum and minimum allocation parameter for each class or style.

2. ***Anticipated Rate of Return.*** Within the AAA will be the projected return rates for each of the asset classes and investment styles. This is challenging as it, in effect, is an attempt to predict the future. Markets traditionally have long periods with both above average and below average rates of return, and these deviations from the overall are seductively misleading. The AAA will rely instead on long-term historical rates of return, coupled with economic forecasting, in arriving at a projected rate of return.

3. ***Realistic Degree of Risk.*** The AAA must not provide a false sense of security to the board, no matter how well reasoned or how much information is included. The board will be reminded in the AAA of the actual degree of risk associated with each asset class and investment style. Drawing on long-term historical data, the AAA will include worst-case scenarios and realistic volatility levels. A track record of above-average performance in one class or style for a prolonged period does not mean that it will be repeated.

4. ***Various Assumptions.*** The time period selected can have everything to do with an historical average. For that reason, the AAA will include a number of time periods and will present a scenario for each of them using various probabilities for the anticipated rate of return and volatility level. These will be used to put the assumptions to the test. The significance is that such an approach puts to rest any thought that the AAA is the result of exact science. It will show the importance of the assumptions and underlying data by producing very different out-comes in various scenarios.

The Existing Portfolio

In preparing an Asset Allocation Analysis, you can start

from scratch, or if the board desires, it can be conducted incorporating aspects of the existing investment program. If starting from a clean slate, the current allocation of asset classes and use of investment styles have no influence on the AAA.

The analysis is based on long-term historical performance of general investment vehicles and economic forecasts as commonly accepted. The analysis also would not reflect the performance of any existing money manager. For that reason, the recommendations would come exclusively from the asset classes and investment styles themselves, independent of the current money managers.

However, if the nonprofit wishes to retain certain portions of their existing investment program, such as a specific money manager, then he or she would be included in the asset allocation.

In cases when a specific money manager is identified for retention, the board might also indicate the percentage of the portfolio assets to be allocated to the manager. If not, the AAA will make a recommendation in that regard. Either way, the AAA will report on the best deployment of the remaining assets to complement the current money manager, consistent with the nonprofit's overall investment objectives.

Rebalancing

Diversification not only applies to the investment vehicles within the portfolio, but is the technique most nonprofits use with money managers. This means they employ the services of several money managers with investment styles that complement the asset classes selected and assigned to them. This is relatively simple in the beginning, but once engaged the actual performance, both of the asset classes and of the money managers, will begin to differ, and often differ substantially, over time. The result is that the careful balance of assets, investment styles and risk goes askew. This is the important reason for earlier establishing the parameters. What is also required is to set in place procedures, that is, a process, for rebalancing the assets when necessary.

Such a process assures that regardless of the performance of any asset class or specific money manager, the portfolio will remain positioned consistent with the nonprofit's established goals. When no set procedure for rebalancing exists there is often a tendency to leave alone whichever asset class or money manager is performing well. When this occurs over time, the class or money manager can come to have an exaggerated presence in the investment program. Or there might be a tendency to simply rebalance the portfolio at random, without regard to its performance or that of the money managers, based on the board's perception of the state of the market.

Neither of these approaches serves the long-term interest of the nonprofit's investment program. As an alternative, the AAA will specify procedures to determine when rebalancing is required and how to go about it. These will include the periodic examination of the market values of the asset classes and money managers. Maximum and minimum parameters, known as rebalancing points, will also be established for each of the target allocations. The purpose is to determine whether any of the rebalancing points have been reached. The rebalancing points and the frequency of reviews differ from nonprofit to nonprofit and must be set individually.

If it is established that a rebalancing point has been reached, then the asset allocation is now significantly different from the established target. At this point, the board must consider whether or not to rebalance the portfolio. If rebalancing is undertaken, it is generally best to review all targets and asset allocations, as it is usually wise to make a number of adjustments at the same time. When those adjustments take place, assets are transferred to bring the portfolio back within its targeted allocation.

No rebalancing is routine. It will have a significant, even

a dramatic, impact on the position of the portfolio in the market. For that reason every rebalancing should be conducted pursuant to an established procedure and be formally approved by the board.

Through such measures an allocation of the nonprofit's assets will be implemented and maintained. This process will assure that the nonprofit is well served and that the portfolio will reflect the optimal rate of return for the established level of risk.

7.
BEHAVIORAL FINANCE

We are all human, all of the time.

It is the nature of most of us to enjoy the sensation of speed, yet on an open expanse of highway we hold to, or close to, the speed limit. We might do so for safety concerns, or because we believe in obeying the law, or because we don't want a ticket. Regardless of our reason, we elect to suppress an all too human tendency.

Late on a spring or summer day, as we gaze out our office window, our human tendency is to leave work and get outside. We even have a name for it: spring fever. But we don't. We suppress our human desire to enjoy nature at its best.

So too should it be when it comes to investing. We must adopt a policy and exercise a strategy that is often contrary to our human impulses. A common human characteristic, though it has its matching opposite, is to want to make the big score, to make money in ways most people do not, to carve out a distinct character for ourselves as individuals who do not follow the pack. Most of us succeed in overcoming this tendency and recognize that while a measure of risk taking is necessary when investing, so too is caution. We understand on an unemotional level that steady and true is the best course.

And so it should be for the board members of charities and nonprofits. They should come to the investment decision-making process with an understanding that while some risk is desirable, it must be controlled and balanced against the wisest long-term course.

Yet, far too often investment decisions are made in a very different way. If we placed our portfolio in funds that matched the S&P 500 from January 1, 1985 through December 31, 2004, according to Dalbar, Inc. in their "Quantitative Analysis and Investor Behavior" Report, 2005, we would have experienced a rate of return of approximately 13.2%. Yet the average investor who places money in these funds sees a rate of return of just 3.7%. How can that be?

The disparity exists because of human nature.

The Psychology of Investing

Why you invest your money *where* you do can tell you a great deal about yourself. In fact, an honest assessment of our finances, something we rarely if ever undertake, could likely tell us everything we need to know about our character and what motivates us.

Even in those situations in which we successfully suppress our emotional and psychological response in making investment decisions, emotions remain an active component for nearly everyone. The reason for this is because money is psychologically charged. When making major financial decisions it is not unusual for people to experience depression, anxiety, hostility and anger, or on the other side, resignation and apathy. Psychosomatic illnesses are not uncommon. Counselors will tell you that couples fight over money decisions as much as they do child discipline and sex. Financial experts report that money, or to be more specific debt, is the leading cause of divorce.

The concept of money is actually far more complex than most realize. Ask almost anyone why a hundred dollar bill, which is after all just a piece of paper, has value and they could not explain it to you. Yet, having money in your pocket and in your bank account is a satisfying experience, just as scrimping your way through the day only to return home to an ocean of debt is a destructive one.

More often than not, it's not about having enough to eat, or clothes on our back – it's about money itself. And so it should come as no surprise that our behavior in regards to money and investments has deeply rooted motivations, many of them concealed from our conscious thoughts, nor should it be surprising that when it comes to money we lie to ourselves – a lot.

Behavioral Factors and Investing

Financial decision-making is to a degree the result of rational thought and knowledge, but it is also the consequence of values, emotions and bias. Though their affects are not fully understood, the stock market is known to often reflect the buying and selling patterns of a mass market driven by individual psychological forces. In fact, a fair degree of market volatility is considered to be the consequence of people behaving a certain way just because that's what others are doing, or because they are following a fad. The spread of certain mass behavior towards the market, either buying or selling, has been compared to that of the spread of an epidemic.

Investors generally believe they act independently of emotional and psychological impulses. They consider themselves to be rational and objective when it comes to making investment decisions. They tell themselves, and others, that they analyze key factors, obtain pertinent information, then make calculated decisions designed to optimize their investment income.

To a certain extent this is very often true. What they do not acknowledge though is the role human psychology, our essential personality, plays in making many of the choices that lead to the final decision. For example, many years ago the investor may have had an unpleasant encounter with a broker at one of the major investment banking institutions. Never mind that they offer superior resources and advice, the investor never accesses any of their information, shutting him or her off from valuable insight.

The reality is that people often make investment decisions that are irrational under examination. They might possess an abundance of information yet still make the wrong choice. In so doing, they miss important opportunities to increase their rate of return and as a result earn less than they might otherwise.

Loss aversion is one of the powerful reasons why individual investors fail to match the rate of return experienced by institutional investors. When the market dips, they sell to avoid a greater loss and in so doing deny themselves the possibility of the greater gains. The same factors, on a much grander scale, led to mispriced stocks and a distortion of the marketplace in general.

Because of this, there exists a new field of research that studies persistent short-term mispricing that leads to long-term adverse consequences. It is called Behavioral Finance and has resulted in great strides towards explaining irrational decision-making by analyzing the emotional, behavioral and psychological components of the process.

It has been found that even small improvements in eliminating behavioral factors from decision-making can have a very positive impact on overall performance. Consider the trained and experienced market analyst. It has been demonstrated that such an analyst has only a slight advantage over the market itself. Often they are only correct just a bit over half the time. But the difference that comes in performance from just that slight advantage is profound. Compounding the extra rate of return over decades produces a far greater rate of return.

Consider a sports analogy. The difference between a baseball batter with a .250 average is not so very much, statistically, from one with a .300 average. Yet the one player will have a short career in the major leagues while the other will have a long, and lucrative, career. And the difference between their performances is only .05%

Or consider the money in a traditional IRA or in a 401K that is tax deferred. Match such a fund to one subject to the income-tax rate and the difference is day from night.

Eliminating, or even reducing, the human behavioral element in investment decision-making will have a profound impact on the future rate of return. It is for this reason that the average institution usually has a much better rate of return on investments than the typical individual. The primary reason for this is that institutions have in place policies and procedures to remove the human element from investment decision-making. One of the reasons why the average 401K investor today is doing so much better than the individual investor did in years past is the advent and use of mutual funds. Mutual funds are institutions which follow an established investment policy in placing their portfolio.

Psychology and Decision Making

The human mind is very complex. It performs an incredible range of functions, both conscious and unconscious. If we lose the use of a portion of our brain, especially when we are young, the remaining portion will tend to perform the lost functions. Rational thinking is only one part of what our brain does. It's an amazing, and poorly understood, aspect of the human condition.

Understandably then, financial decision-making is a very small part of our brain functionality. Psychology plays a role in all of our decisions, even the ones we believe to be most rational. Even experienced and usually objective investment consultants may find their observations about a certain investment vehicle being shaped by a previous loss rather than from a rational analysis of the company.

The reason for this is that each question in a sequence

that leads to a decision is set up, that is, is influenced, by the question and answer just before it. What this means is that a minor alteration motivated by emotion or psychology at the *beginning* of a discussion can magnify itself all out of proportion to the original distortion until a false decision, or at least, a less optimal one, is reached.

Since a minor factor in a series of questions and answers can greatly distort the outcome, behavioral finance researchers addressed the same phenomenon to understand certain persistent market inefficiencies. It is common, for example, for securities to be priced in ways that do not indicate their actual value.

Researchers have developed the following influencing factors:

- Overconfidence
- Anchoring
- Frame dependence
- Loss aversion
- Hindsight biases

Let's take a look at each of them in turn and how they influence what should otherwise be a rational, unemotional decision-making process.

Overconfidence

We tend to be overconfident when making judgments. When people are asked to make a choice then estimate their probability of being right, they tend to believe they are correct eight out of ten times. In fact, they tend to be right seven out of ten times. This may not seem to be much, but consider that small changes in decision-making compounded over a series of decisions has a tremendous impact on the final result. Steer a boat only one degree off the correct bearing for your destination and you will miss it if the voyage is of any significant duration.

It is our nature to give ourselves credit for more virtues

than we possess. This human characteristic is so universal that the occasional individual we encounter who thinks less of themselves stands out from everyone else. It is more typical for us to give ourselves credit for more skill, ability and knowledge than we actually have. This is manifest in us through overconfidence.

Overconfidence, in and of itself, is not a bad thing; in fact, it has its advantages. It allows us to quickly discern conditions around us, it helps us to readily identify patterns from the past and allows us to exploit opportunities. Because of overconfidence we can often act more quickly.

But overconfidence can easily become rashness, and from it stems many behavioral mistakes in our daily lives. There is the finest of distinctions that separate a mistaken hasty judgment from a correct quick decision. When it comes to investment decisions, overconfidence usually results in a failure to properly analyze information and often leads to poor risk assessment.

Even when we guess, we tend to exhibit greater confidence in our answer than is justified by the facts. For this reason, overconfidence is a prevalent risk in making investment decisions because a crucial aspect of the process consists of analyzing a finite volume of information to arrive at accurate forecasts.

Anchoring

Before answering any question our mind instinctively seeks a reference point. This allows us to find a context for the question and from that context comes our response. Behavioral finance analysts call a reference point an "anchor," while the context is referred to as a "frame." We rely very much on anchors and frames to identify and rationalize the information we take in at any given moment, even though neither of them may be based on established facts. Regardless, we use them to interpret information and make our predictions.

Say a traveler is in the American Southwest one summer, having been raised in Seattle, Washington. He hears thunder and looks to the sky. His frame of reference, that is, how and when rain occurs in general, and his anchor, how often it rains when the sky is cloudy and there has been thunder, allow him to make the immediate decision that it is about to rain, and rain for an extended period of time. He hurries indoors and is surprised to see everyone else going about business as usual. In fact, there isn't an umbrella to be seen.

The error he has made is based on his experience, which is true and reliable for Seattle, but does not apply to the specific hot summer conditions of the Southwest where the air is very dry and cloud cover is not extensive or lasting. At most there will be a brief shower, though much of the water will evaporate into the dry desert air before it strikes ground. The sky will be clear within moments. What he expects will not happen.

Analysts would use another example. In mental anchoring we are guided in the specific by general principles we take from our life's experience or by extending events with logic. Consider a tossed coin. Toss it enough times and heads and tails would result exactly fifty percent of the time. This is the principle in general. But in the specific our Seattle visitor might watch a coin tossed, say ten times, and see it land on heads eight times in a row. From that he logically, and erroneously, establishes a mental anchor and concludes the coin is more likely to land on heads the next time it is tossed.

Such conclusions are all too common. Las Vegas and Atlantic City have built enormous, ornate structures and reaped billions in profits depending on this kind of logic. Simply put, people tend to see trends where none exist. They commonly make probability assessments based on relatively small samples, disregarding the reality that long-term performance may not reveal itself over the short term.

Investment consultants are not immune to this human

tendency when they predict the direction of individual investment vehicles or the market in general. The two common errors are a belief that a "trend" will continue, or that it is time for a "trend" to reverse itself. In either case the error is in perceiving a pattern, the "trend," from a short-term phenomenon. The reality, which should be known to the consultant, is that short-term market movements are random and that no trend exists.

Expectations based on early performance often also establish our anchor. Say a company posts record profits and market share for three consecutive years. We "logically" conclude the same thing will happen in the fourth year. Instinctively relying on such an anchor, market analysts routinely misprice stocks.

A proper analysis might reveal excessive debt, market saturation for the product line, increased competition, or any one of a number of factors that point to a sharp downturn, but our anchor leads us to believe that past performance will continue, at least for one more year. The collapse of NASDAQ in 2001 was caused in large part by just such "logic."

<u>Frame Dependence</u>

While anchoring is the danger when believing you are analyzing data, the frame of reference is the pitfall when you make a choice disguised as a prediction. The frame is the way an issue is put. It is a variation of the old saying, "He who frames the question dictates the answer."

Consider it this way: if you come from a volatile, unhappy family as a child, you will tend to expect the same when you have a family of your own. And what we expect becomes our reality.

Many stocks declined in the immediate aftermath of the events of 9/11. Great numbers of these stocks were discounted as much as 30%. Yet as they recovered in subsequent months, investment consultants were slow to recommend acquiring them. Their frame of reference had been rattled and because of that they failed to adequately exploit an investment opportunity. The facts were there, but the context in which they saw those facts had been altered and that adversely affected their judgment.

In such a situation the investment consultant must maintain discipline to be positioned to exploit such opportunities. The lesson to take from frame dependence is to keep broad comparative frameworks in mind whenever analyzing potential investments. It is very, very easy to see only the little picture and lose perspective.

Loss Aversion

For most people, losing hurts more than winning feels good. It's why most people don't gamble very often or risk very much when they do.

This aversion to loss strongly influences investment decisions. Most people will not accept the chance for a 15% gain if there is a matching 15% chance to sustain a loss. Analysts have estimated that the fear of loss is twice as great as any pleasure from making a gain.

What this means is there is a tendency among investors to avoid the possibilities of loss, even though such an approach greatly diminishes the prospects for significant gains. This aversion to loss is a powerful influencing factor in any investment decision-making process.

Hindsight Biases

While these behavioral predispositions influence our decisions about future investments, they are also influencing factors when considering previous data. Just as modern historians churn over past events in light of today's perspective, so too do investors recast what has taken place in their past. Identified biases include:

1. *Recentness.* People tend to view the most recent events

as being more significant and meaningful than those that previously occurred. This is especially the case if the recent event or events have been dramatic or surprising. The effect is to prevent us from putting them in the proper context of a long-term framework. This tendency distorts our consideration of previous performance, and that can cause current and future misjudgments.

2. *The House Money Effect.* Playing with house money has a liberating effect on most investors. In other words, if our investments have done well we tend to be more aggressive and risk-taking with the increase because it is not money we put into the pot. Gains are considered less tangible and less valuable than the money we earned from our work. This returns to the principle that we have a strong psychological response to money. All money, from whatever source, be it our labor or our investments, is and should be of equal value in our mind – but it is not.

3. *Regret.* Regret is a powerful emotion, one that can dog us all our days. It is not uncommon to experience continuing regret for actions or misdeeds that occurred 30 and 40 years ago. So powerful is regret, and the guilt that often accompanies it, that it can become the single greatest influencing factor in our life.

When it comes to investment decision-making, regret can cause even investment consultants to take away the wrong lesson and compound the error by making wrong future decisions. The allure of regret is that we can never know with certainty what a contrary action would have caused. We might very well regret that alternative just as much had it occurred, but since we didn't experience the result of the alternative action no regret is attached to it.

For example, a man regrets he never asked a certain woman out. It would have changed his life. The reality may not have been the experience he fantasizes. She might have said, "No," or they might have had a terrible time together. But he'll never know. Instead, he fantasizes about the life that might have been if only he had asked her out.

Regret is multifaceted. We tend to experience greater regret over near misses than for opportunities that weren't even close. In the one case, we can visualize the outcome, as it was so tantalizingly close. In the other, it was never really a possibility. So we feel regret with the first, but not the second.

We also are inclined to experience greater regret from an action we took that turned out wrong as compared to doing nothing and missing an opportunity. As it applies to investing this means that buying a stock that subsequently falls in value causes greater regret than failing to buy a stock that substantially rises. A realized loss is of greater emotional impact than a lost opportunity.

Take an investor who considered buying Microsoft stock when it released Windows 95. The investor decided at the time that Microsoft had pretty well run its course, that greater competition was looming and that the potential for future gains was limited. Since then he or she's seen the stock continue to rise. Presented with an opportunity to invest in Microsoft today, or to recommend such an investment, the investor may very well be influenced by regret and pass, again.

When investment decision-making is driven by regret it creates a bias against certain actions, even if they are perfectly rational and sound. Such warped hindsight causes misjudgments, usually unconsciously, and those misjudgments can have a severely negative impact on future gains.

The Psychology of Group Decisions

The way we behave as individuals often stands in stark contrast to our behavior in a group. The military, in particular, has long understood how to cause a disparate collection of individuals to behave as a group. There is little battlefield value to be had from close-order drill, but everyone in the military does it as part of their initial training. Moving as one body, marching in step, are time-honored ways to create a feeling of unity within a group. The uniform and standardized grooming requirements are intended to serve the same purpose.

In the military, group consciousness and behavior serve an important function. In tests of small groups it has been established that they usually have a good track record in making certain decisions. For example, when asked to estimate the number of beans in a jar a group of 56 students chose 871 when the actual number was 850, a remarkable level of accuracy and better than 55 of the students estimating individually.

While group consciousness and thinking is important to the military in particular and certain other organizations as well, it is not always desirable. When someone is asked to serve on a charitable board, the assumption is that he or she will bring to the experience their training, experience and individual thinking. The assumption is that a decision reached by the board will be the best possible because each member will draw on those strengths and bring them to the process. But quite often that is not the case.

We've all seen the Western film in which the angry crowd demands the sheriff turn over a prisoner to be lynched. It is called mob violence, or vigilantism. It is group thinking and action at its worst. Such behavior can become too common on any nonprofit board.

For a group to make a more accurate decision three factors must be present:
- Those involved must be unaffected by others' decisions.
- The likelihood of being correct must be independent of the likelihood of everyone else being correct.
- Each participant must be unaffected by the fact that their own vote could be determinative.

If any of these are broken, the effectiveness of a group's decisions quickly declines.

Groups are subject to anchors and frame dependence just as individuals are. The expectation is that members of a group will exchange ideas with each other, bringing something different to the process. The idea is to be certain everything is covered. Errors on the part of any individual are expected to be corrected by the majority.

The reality is quite different. Considering an issue has the tendency to reduce variation. If the group reaches a consensus that variation is diminished. The effect can very easily be to amplify rather than correct the bias of individuals in the group. Groups show an inability to uncover obscure knowledge, even if highly relevant, while focusing instead on the knowledge that is readily available to all, even if irrelevant or off point. Groups are also susceptible to the "cascade" effect, that is, once a strong opinion is articulated it becomes unlikely that anyone will speak against it and what follows is a rush to a decision. An adverse result of the group decision-making process is that each member will be very strongly committed to the outcome, even in the face of subsequent facts to the contrary.

The most significant difficulty of any group, or board, is the risk of polarization and the resulting groupthink. In this, the board ends up adopting a more extreme position than most of them individually held at the start of the deliberative process. Group thinking consists of:

- Consideration of too few alternatives.
- Lack of critical assessment of individual ideas.
- Highly selective information gathering.
- Absence of a contingency plan.
- Actual feelings and opinions are suppressed.
- Bad decisions are rationalized.
- The group creates the illusion of invulnerability.

There are three accepted solutions for reducing group biases:
1. *Use secret ballots.* A secret ballot tends to reduce the likelihood of social pressure on a board.

2. ***Appoint a Devil's advocate.*** Naming someone to take the contrary position can be helpful, but only if it is a position they actually support.

3. ***Respect other board members.*** Openly acknowledge the contributions certain members bring to the process. If someone is trained and experienced in a useful area, that should be openly acknowledged, and his or her opinion given consideration. This tends to overcome the tendency of most board members to believe they know best on any subject.

Behavioral Finance and Investment Consulting

One of the peculiarities of the human condition is that even when we are aware of a failing or susceptibility in our personality, we are often still its victim. If we have a sweet tooth, and know it, we still eat candy. If we indulge our children, and know it, we often still indulge them. And so, too, is our behavior concerning finance and investment decisions. We can understand all of the above, even believe we are unaffected by it, yet still fall prey to our makeup.

The Molecular Consultant can show you ways to profit from aspects of this tendency. For example, knowing that securities can become mispriced over the short-term, he can provide insight to help identify such securities and advise their timely acquisition. While financial markets generally price investments rationally over the long run, identifying the investment opportunities in the short term is an important skill the Molecular Consultant brings to the table.

The influence of behavior on financial decisions has long been recognized by investment consultants, and the industry has set in place certain investment strategies in response to them. They serve as safeguards against the mistakes that can occur because of these behavioral influencing factors. They are:

1. ***Encouraging clients to balance investments.*** An established balanced strategy, and rebalancing strategy,

is perhaps the easiest and most direct means for avoiding the inherent bias in investment decision making. The theory is that investors should not be too dependent on a single type of investing or invested heavily in just one type of assets.

2. ***Build and maintain a diversified investment portfolio.*** Invest with a wide range of styles and maintain that approach in every market condition. Some styles do better than others or suffer less of a loss in certain market conditions.

3. ***Screen money managers' data bases.*** They are regular buyers of mispriced investment vehicles and have in place those vehicles they require to help identify them. Such investments often have a greater rate of return as the market sees their undervaluation and pushes the price up.

4. ***Follow a defined investment strategy.*** An Investment Policy Statement wisely adopted then faithfully adhered to will reduce your tendency to be drawn into short-term market situations. It can serve to remove, or at least minimize, human bias.

5. ***Manage asset portfolios with a knowledgeable team.*** This approach should allow the inclusion of a number of investment perspectives. Each member of the team serves in effect as a check on the others. The use of a team, with its varying approaches, leads to an informational and rational decision-making process that generally eliminates behavioral biases.

Working with the money managers, the Molecular Consultant will help to keep them focused on long-term models that produce greater gains and avoid short-term strategies and overconfidence that lead to participation in the current market buzz as well as loss aversion when the market is down.

He will expose the money managers to the broad frameworks of investment analysis and, when appropriate, arrange for them to meet with a variety of experts. This serves to enlarge the existing decision-making framework, broaden overall investment knowledge, and help them avoid or suppress behavioral biases. Recognition of such behavioral biases and their identification is an ongoing part of the education scheme. He will also assist in identifying those investment vehicles which are undervalued or mispriced through behavioral biases so the nonprofit or charity can benefit from their acquisition.

The Molecular Consultant will assist his clients in benefiting from what is now known and will soon be known about behavioral finance, and will educate the board and managers accordingly. This is a rapidly growing field, producing ever more sophisticated results, which can positively impact financial investment decision-making.

In short, the Molecular Consultant will:

- Assist in establishing an investment strategy which employs a very broad frame.
- Advise that you diversify assets to take into account market fluctuations and trends.
- Advise you invest according to your Investment Policy Statement to exploit certain short-term opportunities and to eliminate, as much as possible, biases from the decision-making process.
- Remind the board of the common influencing factors of overconfidence, distortions caused by mental anchors and frameworks, disproportionate aversion to losses, excessive sensitivity to most recent events and to dramatic or unexpected ones, and the profound effect of regret on the decision-making process.
- Remind and counsel against letting aversion adversely affect future earnings.

Finally, investment processes must be constantly reviewed. Our human nature has an insidious way of taking control of any device we have created to provide an impartial process and warp it to our psychological desires. The more deep-seated the psychological motivation, the more it is concealed from our conscious mind, the more certain we can be that it has affected the very creations we have set in place to thwart it. For this reason, and others, we must constantly reexamine the investment practices and procedures that we have established.

The Molecular Consultant recognizes that every approach to investment contains within it a degree of behavioral bias. If it were purely a numbers game, computers could do it. There is always a human element in making sound investment decisions. Their goal is to understand that bias always exists to one degree or another, to minimize its influence, to educate the board continually to maintain their awareness and to provide the expertise every endowment, foundation, charity and nonprofit deserves.

8.
BLIND RISK MODELING

Understanding risk, its subtleties, its influence and its effect on what we do and on what we wish to do is an important part of the investment process.

In finance, risk means the fluctuations in the value of an investment vehicle. This is typically called volatility, and ranges from very volatile to stable. There are as well different kinds of risk. The general rule as concerns investment risk is that higher risk means greater volatility and with greater volatility comes a greater potential for gain. With lower risk comes less volatility but also a diminished likelihood of gain. In other words, there is always a trade-off between risk and your expected rate of return.

The many solutions for constructing a risk-conscious portfolio which work for a specific investor are only a portion of the process as it applies to nonprofits. There are so many added factors contributing to a nonprofit's risk tolerance that extra measures must be taken to ensure a proper asset allocation.

The Individual and Risk

Risk is an inherent factor in life and whether we realize it or not it exists in all facets of our existence. It is in understanding and accepting risk that we become "risk conscious" rather than "risk fearing," and the difference is often the distinction between the truly successful and the also-rans. An investor who fears risk will never be able to realize the returns of the one who *understands* risk.

In finance, risk is simply a statistic, which like all statistics can be reduced to simple terms. It can then be compiled into large groupings which create statements of probability which are more trustworthy than any instinct could ever be. It is the ability to ignore instinct and follow these probabilities which allows wise investors to make significant gains, while risking no more than those who gain in baby steps.

It is important that investors, especially nonprofit board members, be able to ignore their instinctual fear and follow sound investment advice based on fact rather than emotion.

Biases

There are any number of biases to which people are inclined. We can be aware of these, or unaware of them, but in either case they exercise a degree of influence over our behavior. Some of the most influential biases that affect us in investment decision-making are:

1. *Availability.* When an event is easier to imagine or recall we generally consider it to be more likely to occur. An example of this is the national crime rate. It has been falling steadily for some years, yet coverage of crimes that occur on the other side of the country is now greatly increased with instant reporting on 24-hour cable news shows. In addition, local crime is a staple on the local evening news shows. The result is that most people consider themselves to be more at risk from crime than they really are.

2. *Familiarity.* What we most dread is the unknown. Almost any risk we know is less feared than one about which we have little knowledge. For example, investors generally see greater risk in international vehicles than

the statistics support.

3. *Illusion of Control.* We tend to underestimate risk when we are in control. For example, we are at far greater risk driving our car to the airport than we are flying on a commercial flight, yet we *feel* safer in the car because we have the belief that we are in control.

4. *Mood.* When we feel good, we feel lucky; when we feel bad, we feel unlucky. This affects how we behave during our daily life and it often determines how we make investment decisions.

To one degree or another we are all influenced by our biases. We often allow them to form our opinion and influence our judgment before we even realize it's occurred. More profoundly, they motivate us to act most of all when we deny they exist. This is why understanding them is so important.

Board Psychology

Because every board member is a fiduciary there always exists the likelihood that if things go very wrong for the nonprofit the board members might be held personally liable. Unfortunately, when things go well, which is far more likely, all a board member will reap is praise.

What this means in practice is that no board member wants the nonprofit to lose money. Besides looking bad in others' eyes, there is always the risk of having to defend your actions against accusations of misconduct. So when an investment, or investment policy, goes south, or appears to, there is a tendency for board members to want to bail out quickly. They are, in short, more loss-averse than they are willing to sustain a loss for the likelihood of a future gain. So it is during a difficult market when the influences of behavioral finance most aggressively assert themselves.

The inherent tendency is for board members to "overlay" their personal risk bias when engaged in the management of a nonprofit asset portfolio. This occurs even when the board has been properly educated and understands the predisposition to do so. It's like smoking cigarettes in a way. We can know all about the health problems associated with it, but we step out and light up anyway, comforted by the other smokers around us.

Just as every organization, whether a for-profit or nonprofit, has its own distinct DNA, that is, its own unique character and makeup, so to does every board. The psychology of each board is determined by the psychological influences affecting every board member individually. There is a misguided tendency to consider a board, functioning as an institutional entity, to not be driven by the natural impulses of each individual member.

An important role of the Molecular Consultant is to bring the findings of behavioral finance to board members. This ongoing education is vital. In short, board members often must be prevented from derailing a sound investment plan through their own good intentions, misguided direction or behavioral biases.

All of us are subject to these influences. We like to believe we are not, but that is simply not the case. We are all motivated by complex emotions, past life experiences, the advice of friends and colleagues, and by our own innate character. This is why it is important to set in place those processes that eliminate the human psychological and emotional biases from investment decision-making. Perhaps the most important role of the Molecular Consultant is to that end.

It has been our experience that even when we have carefully explained behavioral finance, that board members often "don't get it." Oh, they hear the words, recognize the behavior in others, but consider themselves personally to be immune, or to have successfully suppressed such motivations. They nod their head and respond appropriately then, often only a few minutes later, when called to participate in a financial decision, take part in it motivated by over-confidence, or regret, or... any of the other factors. The reality is that no matter how well we understand something intellectually, we are still motivated by our emotional makeup, and our ability to conceal that from ourselves is enormous.

Risk and the Fiduciary

The fiduciary has a legal and ethical responsibility to the financial success of a nonprofit through prudent practices. If unethical decisions, or decisions made lacking sufficient information, are made and they have a negative impact on a nonprofit, those in a position of fiduciary responsibility will be held accountable. Mistakes of this kind can, and most likely will, entail legal proceedings and court decisions which can virtually end careers and nonprofits. This is a major source of stress for any fiduciary. The result, very often, is to create an excess of caution when making investment decisions for a nonprofit.

Undue caution actually harms a nonprofit by not allowing it to perform to its full potential. Underperforming can be just as detrimental to a nonprofit as ignoring risk in some instances. The Molecular Consultant will assist the nonprofit in determining its acceptable level of risk. This accomplishes several things, one of which is to eliminate the risk of being overly cautious with nonprofits' investments. To do this he will conduct a study to gather information about each board member's individual risk tolerance. Then, through an in-depth process we call Blind Risk Modeling, he will determine the ideal cumulative risk tolerances for the nonprofit.

Group Dynamics and the Nonprofit

Group dynamics is the branch of social psychology that studies interaction in social groups. When people are part of a group they tend to be influenced by one another in adverse ways and the resulting decisions may not be optimal for the organization. There are many different types of group dynamics which may influence the decision-making of the nonprofit boards. These include:

1. **The Political Model.** This involves the various members of a decision-making body using his or her own viewpoint to create a situation advantageous for his or her own position. The flaw in this type of group dynamic is that not all participants are fully aware of their constituents' knowledge.
2. **The Process Model.** This involves the board making decisions based on precedent and established guidelines. The flaw here is that while a bureaucratic decision-making process may ease things for the decision-makers, in the end it may not be what is best for the nonprofit.
3. **Group Dynamic Shifters.** These are circumstances which change, or shift, the attitudes or mindset of decision-makers when they are in a group. There are two:
   - The "risky shifter" occurs when people meet and are comforted by the task of being part of a group. They tend to disregard danger and are susceptible to taking more risks, because they know they won't suffer the consequences alone. Such behavior can have a detrimental impact on nonprofit decision-making.
   - The "first-shift" occurs during a stalemate in the decision-making process. When a group cannot agree on something, as soon as one individual in that group shifts his or her opinion it is often human nature for each member to join sides with that "first-shifter" in order to come to an agreement. Again, this may not be in the best interests of a nonprofit because the individual who makes the initial decision to shift may not be the one most qualified to do so.

Groupthink, the Theory

Psychologist Irving Janis found that group dynamics can have a significantly negative impact on the way groups make decisions. In 1972, based on such group behavior, Janis created a new theory he termed "groupthink". Janis identified the phenomenon as the kind of thought that people engage in when deeply involved in a cohesive group, when the members' desire for unanimity overrides their motivation to realistically assess alternative courses of action. Groupthink can also be defined as a phenomenon when people seek undivided concurrence in spite of opposing facts pointing to a different decision. According to Janis, groupthink most often occurs on committees or in large organizations.

What this means is that when people meet as part of a group they often make bad decisions. Individual members of a nonprofit board may attempt to conform their own opinion in such a way as to match it to the perceived group opinion, resulting in decisions which aren't really what anybody individually wanted, but that everyone thinks the others want.

Groupthink can have several symptoms to which any nonprofit board is susceptable. The first of these is what is known as the "illusion of invulnerability." This is the false belief that when people gather and make decisions as a group they find it harder to believe they could be wrong because they assume all of their peers in the group are double-checking each other.

Another common symptom of groupthink is a "belief in the inherent morality of the group," which stems from the same source as the illusion of invulnerability. People feel that the group is greater than they are as individuals. As a consequence, they assume a stance that everyone is working together for the "greater good." Since that is the case, their group decisions are inherently moral.

Another symptom of groupthink is "collective rational-ization." This occurs when the group justifies a decision merely because the other members of the group support it. For example, if one board member believes something, then the others will rationalize to themselves that it must be true because so-and-so believes it as well.

Psychologists have also noticed that "out-group" stereotypes can develop as a negative result of groupthink. When these out-group stereotypes exist there tend to be prejudices among the different divisions within a group. This very often includes a lack of respect for the opinions of other group members on nonprofit boards among those who have a greater perceived measure of power than the rest.

A serious symptom of groupthink is the "self-censorship" that often exists when groups are cohesive. This includes people not making known their own ideas, no matter how good or correct they may be, because they want to be a part of the consensus of the group as a whole. This symptom directly correlates to "direct pressure" on dissenters. When someone speaks out in a groupthink environment they are often ostracized for their different opinions or beliefs. This stifles open discussion and can have an incredibly negative effect on a group's decision-making ability.

One of the most important advantages to making decisions in groups is that there are many viewpoints which help to identify or eliminate any faults or flaws in potential decisions. But that advantage is abandoned in a groupthink scenario which can be dangerous to the outcome of decisions.

What many people often do in groupthink situations is assume that there is unanimity, when there may not be. This often leads to group members taking silence to be acceptance, which is not a prudent practice in group decision-making. Group members should question anything they think is wrong; it's why groups can be so useful.

The final symptom displayed by groups that suffer from groupthink is the self-appointing of "mind-guards." Mind-guards are individuals who protect the most important decision-makers from any dissenting ideas or opinions. For example, in a nonprofit this could be someone with expert knowledge or administrative power who notices dissenters among the group and quells their worries before they give strong utturance to them.

Related Decision-Making Problems

Along with the common symptoms of groupthink there are seven specific decision-making problems which are created by their presence. Those seven decision-making problems are:

- Incomplete survey of alternatives
- Incomplete survey of objectives
- Failure to examine risks of the preferred choice
- Failure to re-appraise initially rejected alternatives
- Poor information search
- Selective bias in processing information at hand
- Failure to work out contingency plans

Groupthink and Negative Power

Modern psychologists find examples of decisions that have been negatively impacted by groupthink throughout history. In American history, to name a few, these include the Pearl Harbor bombing, the Bay of Pigs Invasion, the voyage of the Titanic, the Space Shuttle Columbia disaster, and the bankruptcy of Enron.

The most explicit example of groupthink in recent U.S. history is generally accepted to be the Space Shuttle Challenger disaster. The cause of the the shuttle explosion just moments after launch, destroying millions and millions of dollars of research and preparation and, most importantly, ending the lives of seven brave astronauts, was a faulty O-ring seal. The weather was simply too cold for the rubber to properly seal the gaps and contain the explosive force of the rocket engine. The rings had never been tested in such cold conditions but because of groupthink the responsible decision-makers disregarded the concerns of the scientists and engineers involved in that specific part of the mission. The Challenger team exhibited all eight of the symptoms of groupthink in their flawed process which eventually led to the tragic deaths of these American heroes.

Another example of groupthink is the example of the many nonprofit foundations and individuals who fell prey to the Ponzi-scheme of John G. Bennett Jr. of New Era Philanthropy in Philadelphia. The announced concept behind how this was to work was interest-based. New Era Philanthropy claimed it would match the donations of organizations after a certain time period, during which New Era would collect the interest on the principal given to them by donors to cover the costs of running their organization. Many nonprofits fell prey to this fraudulent scheme – and groupthink is largely to blame.

Groupthink occurred on two levels in this instance. The first was from within. Members of boards were influenced by groupthink from amongst themselves, meaning that the board of that nonprofit was acting as the "in-group." The second level included the greater nonprofit industry. This was caused because one board was taken in by the New Era scheme, and subsequently other nonprofits felt justified in doing the same thing. They were all given the illusion of invulnerability simply because they were part of a larger group. When a nonprofit's board saw that a dozen other nonprofits had trusted their money with New Era Philanthropy they assumed it must be a good idea, otherwise those boards wouldn't have chosen to involve themselves.

They were wrong. What followed was a vicious chain reaction which ended on the cover of the *Wall Street Journal* for an entire week in the middle of May, 1995. In all, 185 organizations were duped by Bennett's New Era Philanthropy scam. According to the *Wall Street Journal*, there were red flags raised all over the place. And no one could understand, or explain, how so many intelligent people, controlling so much money, could have been so easily fooled into ignoring these red flags. This is a prime example of how groupthink can have a detrimental impact on nonprofit decision-makers and their organizations.

The Blind Risk Model

Now, while groupthink may not always have as dire an effect on nonprofits as was the case with New Era Philanthropy, groupthink is still a serious problem, one which all nonprofit board members must take into account.

Leading groupthink psychologists have determined that the best way to eliminate the groupthink problem is to use an outside consulting source with the right experience. This process may be tedious and time consuming, but the Molecular Consultant will gladly peform it because it is so vital to the overall success of an investment program.

The Blind Risk Model has been designed to eliminate the groupthink that might potentially occur on a nonprofit board by requiring that all members formulate their conclusions on risk, both on an individual and on a group level. The board members, regardless of the influence they may have, are all considered carefully in the Blind Risk Modeling process. There are many steps to the Blind Risk Model and the reasons behind each are critical to its development. The process takes into account many factors which are essential in determining a proper asset allocation and investment policy statement, while avoiding the problems that can potentially occur.

One of the most important factors which go into creating a successful Blind Risk Model is the weighting system. This serves several functions, but most importantly, it helps a Molecular Consultant determine which board members will tend to influence other members of the board. This aids in dealing with many of the issues created by groupthink.

In order to weight the individual board members, a Molecular Consultant will conduct in-depth surveys and interviews. He will essentially create a resume for all of the members of the board. This will allow the Molecular Consultant to determine who knows what and how each opinion should be weighted in making specific decisions. For example, if certain members of the board have experience in investing in stocks [perhaps at one point in their lives they were analysts or stock brokers] then those members should have a slightly higher weighted opinion than others when dealing with investing in the stock market.

If the other members of the board are aware of the experienced individual's knowledge of the subject matter of the decision at hand, they will also be more likely to blindly trust them. This is not good. Blindly trusting anyone in a strong cohesive group environment often leads to poor decision-making.

The Molecular Consultant will be aware of these pitfalls and be able to make the board aware of them as well. Also, as an outside source, he will be able to identify solutions that lead to optimal decision-making.

The Molecular Consultant Questionnaire

Our experience has taught us that we need to know a great deal more about each board member, and for that reason we do not rely on the traditional risk questionnaire. When the chips are down, when the stock market has a sharp decline, when the best laid plans for a productive asset portfolio fall on hard times, our experience has been that people turn to their personal risk tolerance in making decisions for the nonprofit. Because of this we solicit information in three vital areas:

- We first want to understand a board member's personal risk tolerance. How would he or she manage his or her own money? How would he or she react to certain events that occur from time to time in the stock market? In adverse times, would the board member step up to the plate, act on strong convictions, or would he or she flee from the decisions previously made? Would the member increase the portfolio's position or would he or she want to sell and take the loss?
- We also want to understand the reasons *why* the member is serving on the board, as this can greatly influence investment decision-making. What are some of the psychological benefits he or she receives from this service? How long do they intend to serve? How does he or she view the organization, and especially, how does he or she view the other board members?
- Finally, we seek to identify who will be the key decision-makers on the board. Who possess the strongest personalities? Who will have the most

influential voice [leaders] and who will be the
listeners [followers]?

Now the Molecular Consultant can more accurately
gauge the process that will take place when hard times come,
as they always do. We will have a better sense of which way
the board will be inclined to move, and who is most likely to
exercise the greatest control in arriving at that decision.

From this information, we are able to extract an
aggregate score. Once we have this number we run two asset
allocation models. One is a typical mean variance optimization model that every proficient financial institution
provides. The second is a downside risk model; that is, how
much can the board really handle when the market goes
down? This is useful in many ways, but especially so in
selecting managers who are appropriate to the investment
goals of a nonprofit and who will not derail the investment
model.

Power on the Board

The process of conducting surveys and interviews will help
the Molecular Consultant to determine which board members
serve which functions for the nonprofit. There are essentially
three types of power which tend to exist on nonprofit boards.
These are:

1. *Expertise Power.* Those with expertise power are individuals
   who have experience in related fields. For our purposes we
   deem those who have experience in investing fields board
   members who hold "expertise power."
2. *Contributory Power.* Those on the board with contributory
   power consists of members who were given a position on a
   board because of their experience in the nonprofit world as
   donors. These individuals have done their part as generous
   givers and in doing so have earned the right to sit on boards
   so that they may be able to help in the decision process. This
   is important if for no other reason than that their money, as

well as that of other donors, is being controlled by the decisions being made. They have the right to participate.

3. *Gavel Power.* This group most often consists of only the chairmen of the board, though in very large organizations there may be several members who have gavel power. These are the board members who sit at the heads of the tables, those who officiate meetings and those who are the public face of the nonprofit. Those with gavel power often have both expertise power and contributory power as well. This group is often weighted higher than the others.

The Molecular Consultant will come to understand the decision-making process in great detail, and will also know how board members interact with one another and know precisely how they fit into the structure of the nonprofit.Once identified, the next step in the process is to determine how these fit into the Blind Risk Model. Understand that these groups never know who they are. The Molecular Consultant doesn't walk into a meeting and tell those with expertise power to raise their hands. It doesn't work like that.

Once it has been determined how the members fit into the nonprofit's board, the weighting process can begin. The process consists of comparing all of the individuals on the board and their various experiences and expertise. For example, those with gavel power are often weighted higher because they usually have the ability to sway decisions, while those with contributory power may be weighted lower.

The process of the Blind Risk Model is of great value here because someone with contributory power may be donating large sums of money to the nonprofit and therefore be unjustly influencing the decision-making of the board. The weighting process properly determines how much of an influence this power should have, based on how well they can make a decision, rather than how they are viewed by other members of the board or how much influence they believe they should have.

Board Members and Risk Tolerance

Once the weighting system is determined, then the Blind Risk Model is completed. The model consists of determining the indivual risk tolerances of board members in two scenarios. The first is their individual risk tolerances, the second is their risk tolerances as board members.

The two are viewed together and through careful analysis are properly combined into what each individual board member contributes to the risk tolerance of the overall board. It is at this stage that the model becomes largely computer based. The values for each board member are entered into a model created by a consortium of computer-modelling experts and financial advisers specializing in nonprofit investment management and consulting.

Along with those values are entered the requirements of the nonprofit, such as fundraising needs, legal limitations, grant and gifting requirements – essentially everything that is at all related to finance for nonprofits. The model, through various mathematic functions, develops a precise and accurate risk tolerance for the nonprofit as an organization. This model is then linked directly to a program which determines proper asset allocation and specifies the investment vehicles which the nonprofit should be pursuing based on their newly discovered optimal risk tolerance.

The Blind Risk Model is a crucial aspect of the investment process for nonprofits. Much time is needed to thoroughly complete it, but any time and effort both on the side of the board and the Molecular Consultant, is well worth it. There have been far too many nonprofits that have derailed a good investment plan out of fear of underperforming.

There always have been and always will be inconsistencies in the market. Variables which cannot be predetermined should not change the way a nonprofit is invested. At times, small adjustments may need to be made, but the overall direction of the portfolio should stay the same for as long as the needs of the nonprofit remain unchanged.

The Blind Risk Model is the best way for a nonprofit to maintain an optimal course and is an assurance to all boards which subscribe to one. The Blind Risk Modeling process is a proven means for eliminating the problems of groupthink, for maintaining a steady course with investments and for aiding in its growth.

9.
INVESTMENT POLICY STATEMENT

While process measures can, and should, be adopted to eliminate or diminish personal and group bias, one of the most important devices for accomplishing this is the adoption and implementation of an Investment Policy Statement, or IPS.

The IPS is the governing document for a nonprofit as relates to investment decisions. A properly drafted Investment Policy Statement will establish a framework for evaluation and monitoring of the existing portfolio, set in place the blueprint for making all investment decisions, and assist in the retention or termination of money managers responsible for specific portfolio accounts.

The IPS also states the assumptions and expectations for the performance of the various money managers. In addition, it provides the policies and procedures; that is, the processes that are to guide investment decision-making and portfolio review. It will also address the administrative and other substantive issues relating to the investment program and is designed to make communication concerning the portfolio and asset allocation easier and more comprehensible.

Overall, a properly drafted Investment Policy Statement once adopted will greatly assist any charity or nonprofit in directing its investment program. Every IPS should include:

- The policies and procedures that the nonprofit will

follow throughout the investment process.

- Issues which may affect the investment program, as well as issues that impact specific areas of investment.
- A blueprint for investing.
- A framework for evaluation.
- A system which aids in the communication and understanding between the individuals and groups involved in the investment process.
- Formal documentation of all issues involved in an investment program.

Lacking such a document as the Investment Policy Statement makes it very difficult, perhaps impossible, to determine if the performance of the portfolio money managers is acceptable, if the portfolio is positioned properly, or even if it is on target to achieve the nonprofit's long-term financial goals.

IPS Functions

It is generally held that the IPS serves at least three important functions:

- It assists the board, the nonprofit managers and the money managers in directing and pursuing the investment goals.
- It provides a window into the investment strategy and policy of the nonprofit to donors and potential donors.
- It assures regulatory authorities and rating organizations that the nonprofit is conducting its investment affairs pursuant to a formal policy against which its performance can be effectively judged.

An IPS defines objectives and goals, outlines methods for achieving those goals, sets regulations and guidelines, specifies risk tolerance levels, prepares timeframes along which goals should be met, and prepares nonprofits for dealing with any changes along the way. A properly prepared Investment Policy Statement will provide the information and guidance needed to make sound investment decisions and set in place the necessary framework for required evaluations.

Because nonprofits are unique organizations, every IPS must be individually tailored. A Molecular Consultant and nonprofit board can develop the optimal IPS for the nonprofit without great effort, so long as several issues are kept clearly in mind. One of the most important aspects of the IPS is the actual investment policy, meaning the risk tolerances and asset allocation of the nonprofit. This portion of the Investment Policy Statement should contain a detailed summary of the conclusions reached through the Blind Risk Model and the asset allocation elements of the consulting process.

While a general statement concerning the nonprofit's investment objectives is helpful, what is also required is a narrative with sufficient detail to provide essential guidance in quantifying more specific objectives and the parameters or targets for them.

A comprehensive IPS will cover a wide range of relevant issues. Some of these concern the financial well being of the portfolio in general, while others will relate to the role of money managers and the issues concerning their performance specifically. Different portions of the IPS will be designated for each issue. Those relating to the portfolio and its functioning will be prepared in conjunction with the board, while the issues concerning money managers will be developed through contact with them.

Achieving the nonprofit's investment objectives is important, but so too is maintaining each board member's fiduciary responsibility. It is not uncommon when an investment program has failed to reach the desired objectives, and complaints are raised, for a review of conduct by an enforcement agency to focus on the process that produced those results. A properly prepared IPS is of assistance in that regard in two ways:

- The fact that the board has addressed the key issues required for an IPS results in an improved process and usually produces a better outcome.
- The mere existence of the IPS confirms that the board sought to fulfill its fiduciary responsibilities and is operating through an established process.

Resolving key issues when drafting the IPS is itself an important component of their fiduciary responsibility and of the portfolio management process. Among others, these include the nonprofit's spending policy, asset allocation, and rebalancing policy. If the board is dissatisfied with any of these, those issues they must be satisfactorily resolved before drafting of the IPS begins.

Benefits of the Drafting Process

The actual process of researching, then adopting an IPS, is extremely useful to the nonprofit as it compels that important long-term decisions be made, or if already made, requires that they be reexamined. For example, who will manage what aspects of the portfolio? What percentage of the assets will be placed into what types of investment vehicles? How much does the nonprofit actually require to fulfill its mission? How much can it reasonably expect from donors? Based on that, what is the ratio of risk to gain to be? Who will administer the investment process within the nonprofit, and how will the necessary information be provided to the board and managers? What constitutes a conflict of interest?

These are just a few of the vital decisions that have to be made and for which a consensus must be achieved before a single word of the Investment Policy Statement is drafted.

When it comes to money at this level, nothing is easy. There is too much to be gained and too much potential risk for any of the required decisions to be simple. Personalities will come in conflict, differing opinions will arise, and it is at such times that board members will be sorely tested. But from the drafting process itself can come a strongly united board with a firm grasp of the financial issues the nonprofit faces. Leaders will have been identified as will those with life resources to bring to the process.

One of the key aspects of the IPS is to define the relationship between those making the specific investment decisions and the board. The roles will clearly emerge and the inherent confusion that typically exists when financial decisions are made on an *ad hoc* basis, as they often are prior to the adoption of the IPS, will disappear with a well-deserved sigh of relief. From disorder comes order, to everyone's benefit.

Through the IPS the board establishes its investment policy and the money managers follow that policy in the real world of daily finance. This is as it should be. Day-to-day financial decisions should be within the province of the account money managers, while policy and oversight belong with the board.

Once it is adopted and set in place, the IPS becomes a working document that is routinely consulted when new situations arise. It is also a historical document that explains the nonprofit's investment strategy, goals, purpose and conduct of the investment program to those outside the nonprofit as well as to new board members.

The Categories

Another way of considering an Investment Policy Statement is to say that it refers to all of the documentation required to address significant, procedural or administrative issues about any portion of the nonprofit's investment strategy. While a carefully crafted and thorough IPS will cover a host of issues, there are certain categories which must be included. These are:

1. ***Specific goals and objectives.*** This includes the definitions, metrics and priorities established for risk and gain, and the applicable timeframes, including those for periodic and regular evaluations of each individual account.
2. ***Managing the portfolio.*** This will include the issues of asset allocation, investment style, what is permitted and what is prohibited, and other issues such as social responsibility in selecting investment vehicles. Delineated are investment targets, variance ranges, and the rebalancing procedure to be followed when the portfolio deviates significantly from the established targets.
3. ***Investment administration.*** This defines responsibility and control over the various aspects of the investment program. It sets communication protocols and establishes how various account details are to be consolidated. The defined system is intended to avoid confusion and allow proper focus on the management of the investment portfolio.

The IPS Advantages

One of the most important processes for the nonprofit with which the IPS is concerned is the search for and selection of money managers. The details for selecting managers are a crucial part of the IPS. This ensures that money managers are selected prudently and consistent with the goals of the nonprofit.

Another reason why an IPS is so necessary for a nonprofit is because there are non-financial issues on which boards must focus. It's true that money and how it's invested are very important to every nonprofit, but having a sound IPS in place means that fiduciaries are more likely to quickly, and responsibly, make investment decisions without diverting valuable time and energy from the mission of the nonprofit.

The Investment Policy Statement will be provided to a

nonprofit's current donors and those from their pool of potential donors. We have found that as a result, the tendency is for donations to increase. The reason is that the IPS provides donors and potential donors with documented proof of the legitimacy and success of the fiduciary practices of the nonprofit. When donors are reassured, by evidence substantiated through fact and documentation, they are much more comfortable in making donations.

The Objectives

An investment Policy Statement is also how investors protect their portfolio from themselves. It does this by keeping investments on track regardless of the periodic "blips on the radar" which often cause an investor needless concern. The well-drafted IPS serves as a bedrock from which investment decisions will be made and in such times will minimize the tendency to react spontaneously to an adverse market condition.

An important function of the well-drafted IPS is that it is one of the best ways to eliminate the problems of groupthink psychology. It is also the best way to minimize the conflicts that may arise on any board.

It is always difficult to keep an eye on every aspect of a portfolio. Attention in a nonprofit is typically focused on fundraising and in distributing income to serve the nonprofit's mission. How accounts are being managed, and the direction of the portfolio can be overwhelming in both detail and in general. Since most nonprofits will have several money managers and employ different investment styles, the need is all the more demanding.

In some instances there are specific requirements for an Investment Policy Statement. For example, retirement accounts are governed by the Employee Retirement Income Securities Act, or ERISA. ERISA mandates that all retirement portfolios be governed by an Investment Policy Statement. ERISA also dictates which components must be present in the IPS. These include a plan to diversify the assets, monitor performance, control expenses and avoid prohibited transactions.

The Issues

A comprehensive IPS will cover a wide range of relevant issues. Different portions of the IPS will be designated for each issue. Those relating to the portfolio and its functioning will be prepared in conjunction with the board, while the issues that will concern the money managers will be developed through contact with them.

Being as specific as reasonably possible ensures that the conduct of the nonprofit's investment policy will go smoothly. It also ensures cohesion among the investing aspects of the nonprofit.

Legal issues which can potentially confront a nonprofit are also included in the IPS. These can include local or national laws which govern the aspects of a nonprofit's operation. There will also be a statement that the fiduciaries are aware of their duties and responsibilities. The fiduciary should understand that he or she may delegate the decisions of his finances to other professionals or trustees, but that no fiduciary can ever abandon the responsibilities of the position. This includes determining goals, allocating assets, establishing an investment policy, approving all investment vehicles, monitoring the performance of assets, and avoiding conflicts of interest.

Because all of the restrictions and regulations are included in a single section in the IPS, regulatory questions are more easily resolved. Another positive result of placing any regulatory and legal issues in an IPS is that if legal action is taken against the nonprofit they have a document establishing that they were aware of, and following, the laws and regulations regarding their conduct.

The IPS will typically also include a history of the nonprofit. This section will describe how and why the founders created it; that is, define its historical mission by stating what the nonprofit was intended to accomplish at the time of its inception. This is important, especially during the early stages of the adoption process. By formally stating the history of the nonprofit, board members and consultants alike will become aware of, and dedicated to, preserving the intentions of the nonprofit's original donors and leaders. With this in mind, what follows will become a continuation of the original dream which now, with the help of modern investment techniques and under the expert guidance of a Molecular Consultant, will be realized and hopefully surpassed.

Often going hand-in-hand with the statement of the history of the nonprofit, an IPS will cover its mission as well, since they are so closely related. This typically includes the mission stated by the founders, the motivation behind that mission, and the financial means through which that mission can be accomplished. The mission statement helps to reaffirm the philanthropic approach of nonprofits, and allows boards and consultants to focus the investment objectives on a single outcome. This is the final realization of the original mission statement of the founders of the nonprofit along with any added missions which may have been adopted during its history.

Objectives

The IPS should then address the scope of investing. This includes the areas of investment which are allowed under the decisions of the board, largely based on asset allocation analysis, risk tolerances, and regulatory restrictions. More than simply specifying just what a nonprofit *can* invest in, this section should encompass all investment vehicles in which the nonprofit *cannot* invest.

An Investment Policy Statement should also cover the objectives and policies of the nonprofit. They are grouped because they often go hand-in-hand. The policies are the means through which the objectives are met, and they both need to be tailored to match one another. Defining the objectives of an organization's investments is crucial to the effectiveness of the IPS and the success of the nonprofit.

These objectives should include those the board deems important enough to be included, and are typically listed in the IPS in priority order. The range of topics comprising the objectives and policies section of an IPS can be far-reaching, but this section is important and is often the greater part of the IPS.

The objectives may be laid out to help meet the needs of the investment program, minimizing risk of sharp declines in value, maximizing returns, generating selected levels of income, having assets exceed liabilities. Many components must be considered to meet the needs of the nonprofit. These also include liquidity, preservation of capital, stability of returns, long-term capital growth, annual returns, and current income.

This section typically includes the objectives and policies of the finances, control, asset protection, and major risks of a nonprofit. The financial objectives and policies section should clearly specify the general aspects of the finances of the nonprofit. This often includes, but certainly isn't limited to:

- Reporting techniques, most typically a quarterly report, including financial positions and financial operating results. This can be provided by a treasurer, but the Molecular Consultant will also provide in-depth quarterly reports or reports with any reasonable frequency that the board may require.
- Debt pay-back methods and objectives.
- Conflicts of interest to be avoided.

The purpose is to ensure that the ongoing financial condition of the nonprofit is consistent with the priorities approved by its board.

The IPS and Asset Allocation

Investment Policy Statements also cover the nonprofit's asset allocation policies. This includes the findings of the Asset Allocation Analysis which the Molecular Consultant conducted. This portion of the IPS outlines in great detail the nucleus of a nonprofit's investment strategy which states precisely what ratio of different investment vehicles the nonprofit will follow.

This is of greatest importance when financial markets shift and many nonprofit board members may become concerned and express a desire to make an immediate change. In such a situation, the reality is that change is very likely the worst possible course of action for the portfolio. Derailing a sound and reasoned investment strategy in response to short-term changes in the market is one of the worst investment decisions any nonprofit or investor can make.

This section of the IPS outlines how to diversify the portfolio and also provides documented proof that your nonprofit has a plan and is sticking to it. It outlines the risk tolerances that the Molecular Consultant will have worked so hard to establish. It is here, in the asset allocation strategy section of the IPS, that the painstaking work of weighting the board members and determining the optimal risk tolerance of the nonprofit will finally be realized. This is the conduit through which risk tolerance becomes more than a concept. The asset allocation section of the IPS brings theory into practice and sets the investment on the optimal track.

The IPS and Risk

The Investment Policy Statement also helps to reduce risk by discussing the problems that may arise internally and cause issues with the investment of a nonprofit's funds. This ensures you are prepared for any eventuality which may affect investments and can include:

- Loss of key personnel, such as any directors or board members.
- Loss of performance or administrative facilities.
- Succession planning to establish what to do when board members step down and end their tenure.
- Establishing a reserve funds system suitable to the needs and goals of the nonprofit.

Many nonprofit Investment Policy Statements also include a section about standards of care. This includes a delineation of prudence, ethics or potential delegations of authority. It specifies how prudence is to be used by those responsible for investment decisions and declares that they shall conduct themselves in accordance with the Prudent Investor Rule in managing the portfolio. The ethics statement usually restates the issues of conflict of interest in more colloquial terms.

Risk, Return and Money Manager Retention

The Investment Policy Statement will establish certain return objectives in the various investment categories. These play a key role in determining which money manager is doing well and which is not. For that reason, if no other, return objectives will be a subject of intense examination during the adoption process. Whether one manager is retained or let go is greatly affected by the objective that was originally specified.

Consider also that no metric ever provides a complete picture by itself and it is for this reason the IPS will allow different types of measurements. These can include nominal and real return targets, a manager universe, a reference benchmark or a primary benchmark. These will allow him or her a means to more fully explain the performance of the account he or she manages.

The key to this approach is to establish which metrics are

best suited for the nonprofit. There are generally three considerations in terms of measurements:

- They must be compatible with the money manager's investment style.
- They must be compatible with the nonprofit's investment goals.
- They must be properly prioritized.

Evaluating return is relatively simple when compared to the next step, which is evaluating risk. It is one thing to establish the risk tolerance in the IPS, quite another to witness it in action. A money manager may employ a wide range of complex, statistical risk variables and it is too easy to become bogged down in them. Often they will have very little to do with the nonprofit's actual risk tolerance. Keeping it simple is generally best. For the board itself, risk is usually measured in just two ways:

- Achieving the targeted return.
- The likelihood of sustaining a significant loss over a specified timeframe.

Finally, it is in considering the rate of return and matching it to objectives where the decision to retain a money manager is usually made. It is never easy, but a sound IPS will encourage a proper discussion relating to retention by setting appropriate standards for evaluation, standards known to everyone from the beginning.

It is here too the admonition to the fiduciary should be kept in mind that his or her loyalty is to the beneficiary of the trust and no other consideration must be taken into account.

The Benefits

These are typically the main aspects of an Investment Policy Statement. Every nonprofit is unique and this should be reflected in the IPS. In theory, an IPS should be like snowflakes, no two should be identical. Some Investment

Policy Statements will be longer than others, some will emphasize legal issues, some will be more dedicated to asset analysis, while some will pay attention to the inner workings of the nonprofit. What matters is that the IPS is tailored to fit the precise needs of each.

The creation of an Investment Policy Statement is no easy task, but is necessary for the success of any portfolio. The Molecular Consultant will certainly ease the burden of creating this document by taking the reins and not only seeing to the tedious details but also in guiding the board through the entire process.

It is not possible to retain an outside consultant and have him or her prepare your IPS in a few short days, then report it back to you, ready to go. The process simply doesn't work that way. The Molecular Consultant will involve the board throughout what is always a time-consuming procedure. The board will never be in the dark on anything. Every decision will involve its input, because without it an IPS won't reflect the specific needs of the nonprofit. He will aid in this process by eliminating any conflict which may arise so as to create a genuine consensus among the board.

The process of preparing an Investment Policy Statement compels nonprofit boards to study matters that had been previously overlooked, and then establishes policies which deal with those concerns directly and explicitly. A nonprofit board conducting business without an Investment Policy Statement has no meaningful investment policy. Without a written and explicit statement of investment objectives all actions conducted by a nonprofit board are merely expressions of undefined concepts. For this reason and others, an Investment Policy Statement is the single most essential document your nonprofit will produce and implement. It is the foundation and framework for the financial success of your nonprofit, or any organization with assets to invest, for that matter.

10.
MONEY MANAGER SELECTION

For all our efforts to make a science out of investing, it still remains a very human process. For this, and other reasons, the people you include in your portfolio management are as important as the procedures and strategies you adopt through the Investment Policy Statement. Just as not everyone is appropriate to serve on the board, so too not every money manager is a good fit. This is just one reason why the selection of your money managers is so important. What should emerge from the selection process is a money manager who is a good match to the nonprofit's investment strategy and objectives.

A money manager, also known as an investment manager or portfolio manager, is the individual who manages the securities of an individual or institutional investor. He is usually employed by an institution which is in the business of managing investment accounts. Money managers often employ many individuals who are specialists in their fields, and by combining their resources are able to manage portfolios very efficiently.

The Goal

In general a mid-sized nonprofit will have six to 10 money managers; optimally, each will possess an area of expertise and experience that suits your nonprofit's investment goals. The primary objective of the selection process is to obtain the best possible manager for each asset class with the expectation that the nonprofit will obtain optimal performance.

Finding the right money manager is not as easy as determining who has the best track record. Every professional has good and bad periods, and so it is for money managers. Given their area of expertise, and state of the market at different times, they can have very good periods and those that are less than stellar. But the goal remains to find the best person for the job.

To make this possible, no artificial constraints should be placed on the search. There must be the expectation, and realization, that you will gather all pertinent information, be objective in evaluating it, and that you will set aside emotions and psychological factors during the process and in making the final determination.

Selecting the right money manager can be time consuming and often requires a good deal of focus from the board and its consultants. In order to make a successful selection process, a nonprofit must have well-established investment goals, a comprehensive database of money managers and of their performance, and the specialized knowledge that goes with selecting the appropriate money managers to match the nonprofit's investment objectives.

The time and effort required to select the right money managers is crucial to achieving your nonprofit's goals. The wrong money manager, or a mismatch between a money manager and the investment objectives, can lead to a decrease in portfolio performance or an unacceptable increase in risk. Hiring the wrong one also often leads to administrative difficulties and expenses that come from the untimely release of a money manager.

The actual process of selection will largely flow from the criteria you set. You are looking for investment style, investment class experience, integrity and reliability, previous success in rate of return, decision-making, consistency, timeframes and history of investment volatility within them. There are also occasionally legal issues to be satisfactorily resolved. The judgment exercised in these and other areas is essential to a proper choice.

Attention must be given during every step of the search and selection. The essential components of a good manager search include:

- An objective review of a comprehensive database of money managers to define a complete list of appropriate options.
- Application of a set of well-defined, quantitative and qualitative attributes.
- A focus on money managers who consistently follow the desired, and permissible, investment styles.
- Evaluation of factors beyond basic performance.
- A comprehensive comparative analysis of all managers.

The primary two steps in finding the right money manager consist of a comprehensive search followed by a careful evaluation of all candidates.

The Search

If the Investment Policy Statement is well crafted, then the job of selecting the money managers will be much easier. Generally speaking, money managers can be placed into an investment style based on how they manage their accounts. Money managers work in all asset classes and in all sizes. Some are focused on fixed-income investments whereas others deal primarily with stocks. The portfolio asset allocation should define the ratio of stock investments to bond investments, as well as specify the nature of those investments, including both domestic [U.S.] and international. Some money managers specialize in growth stocks, others in value. Some money managers focus on large market capitalization companies while others focus on mid or small cap. Many managers invest across several of these; for example, a value manager might invest across the entire market capitalization range, or a small cap manager may invest in both growth and value securities.

Another decision which must be made is whether to invest with an active or passive manager. An active manager strives to surpass the market index, while a passive manager's goal is to match the market index.

While it is important to know which style is associated with which candidate, you should keep in mind that managers change styles, and even when they don't, they often can't be identified with a single category and attempts at pigeonholing tend to be counterproductive. Given such limitations, identifying a money manager with a specific style is an aspect of the process which should not be overvalued.

Once you are aware of the large number of options available to any nonprofit, it is clear why the IPS was created with such specific requirements, and why a Molecular Consultant is so essential to the process.

The Database

The first step in the actual search is to construct an extensive database of potential managers who fit the requirements of the nonprofit. Criteria are then applied to the database and mismatched managers are removed from the list of possibilities. Managers who lack a desired investment philosophy, staff, plan, performance history, or infrastructure are also removed from the list. At this point the list should be culled to a manageable number from which as many managers as dictated by the size of your nonprofit will be chosen. With the parameters clearly set, these can objectively be removed from the database.

As provided in the Investment Policy Statement, any outside consultant utilized by the board for any portion of this process must not have a connection or affiliation with any of the money managers or money manager firms. Obviously, we are of the opinion that a Molecular Consultant is best positioned to perform this service. The Molecular Consultant will be unbiased in assisting in the search and subsequent evaluation. Both the search and the evaluation will be conducted and prepared confidentially to enhance their objectivity. The money managers under consideration will not even be told the name of the nonprofit considering them.

Gathering a list of appropriate money managers is a function often performed by the Molecular Consultant. In fact, there's a good chance that he or she has dealt with some of them before, or at the very least is familiar with them from an earlier search and selection process. Having dealt with the selection process previously gives the Molecular Consultant a great advantage. From the initial vast pool now remains a manageable number of candidate money managers ready to be evaluated.

The Evaluation

The Molecular Consultant will analyze the performance numbers of the remaining money managers. The basic historical performance of money managers is not the most prudent method for selecting managers; hindsight does not work as well in investing as it does in other aspects of life. But nonetheless, appropriate analyses of prior performance numbers allow you to cull the list even further.

Evaluating the candidates begins with a lengthy consultation with the Molecular Consultant during which he collects a wide-range of relevant information. These should ideally take place at his or her office where the candidate is most comfortable and can more fully relate his or her history. It is important to keep in mind that there is no correlation between being glib and making sound investment decisions. Still, you will want a money manager able to effectively communicate verbally.

A Molecular Consultant will look for signs in a manager's past performance. One of these is consistency. If managers are inconsistent in their returns it is more likely that even if they have performed well recently, you risk investing at the end of a hot streak and losing money. Another aspect of performance that will be considered is the measure of a money manager's return relative to the amount of assumed risk.

This process can be quite complicated, but the return on the time and effort by the Molecular Consultant is invaluable and will serve to further effectively cull the list of possible money managers.

Investment Style and Benchmarks

Since Money managers do tend to associate with a specific asset category, comparing a candidate against the accepted benchmarks of his asset category can be very helpful, but while it is a means for establishing the level of risk identified with a specific manager, many experts caution against depending on it excessively. Some money managers are unwilling to assume much risk and limit themselves to benchmark investments because they fear taking risks that might adversely affect their performance and make it more difficult for them to acquire new clients. These will tend to be very conservative in their approach and while they are unlikely to perform below the benchmarks, they are also not likely to exceed it significantly.

Others who deviate more often or aggressively from the benchmarks should not be judged too harshly if they have under-performed over short timeframes. They are working to provide a greater than average rate of return and the timeframe used for the comparison can skew results enormously.

You should also keep in mind that the benchmarks themselves are often changed over various timeframes, making direct comparisons more difficult and less reliable. It is also not unusual for the best money managers to manage portfolios for which no good benchmark is available. They bring their unique approach which is not initially shared by the majority. It only serves to remind that benchmarks are just one tool in evaluating potential money managers, and again one that should not be overvalued.

The Individual Analysis

Once the evaluation of the candidate money managers is complete, a detailed written analysis for each manager's investment style, rate of return, risk and risk-adjusted returns is prepared. It will also include those issues, if any, that are the result of the firm's structure and organization. The way the analysis is presented will facilitate comparison among the various candidate money managers.

In addition, the analysis will include appropriate benchmarks which can be used to evaluate the relative performance of the money managers. The analysis will also compare each candidate money manager against a peer group of managers with the same investment style.

Regardless of the number of money managers under consideration, the written analysis typically consists of seven categories. These categories are:

1. *The Overview.* This will detail the screening process, describe how the pool was created, the objectives of the money manager evaluation and offer a summary of those issues important to each candidate money manager's style, structure and performance.

2. *Money Manager Vita.* This contains the money man-

ager's profile, performance composite and necessary descriptive information.

3. ***Investment Style.*** This includes the particular investment style and philosophy of the candidate money manager. It analysis each money manager in consideration of their overall rate of return, including both return based style analyzes and fundamental style analysis.

4. ***Return.*** This lists the return the money manager has secured and compares it to the appropriate benchmark and money manager peer group. Included will be a comparison during various timeframes and under different market conditions.

5. ***Risk.*** Over a statistically significant timeframe, this considers volatility, overall market performance, and an analysis of various risk factors.

6. ***Return to Risk.*** Employing various accepted ratios, this includes a statistical analysis of the candidate money manager's return as compared to degree of risk.

7. ***Evaluation.*** This is a summary evaluation of the candidate money managers, providing a grade based on the comprehensive selection criteria that have been employed. It permits a peer ranking with the other candidates.

The Mix and Number

Diversification does not relate strictly to the nonprofit's portfolio. It also applies to the number and kinds of money managers it utilizes. Ideally, the nonprofit will want a mix of money managers with different, even contrasting, investment styles and philosophies. This is just one reason why attempting to pigeonhole a money manager into a certain style is not as desirable as it might first appear. They also should bring to the portfolio a wide range of experience and expertise. A mix in gender, artificial as that seems, and in age can also be useful.

There is no magical means for selecting the optimal

number. Six to 10 money managers tends to be average and works for most nonprofits, but a smaller number of highly regarded managers can also be effective, as can a larger number with a greater degree of specialization. What is important is that the mix and number is the right one for your nonprofit, and that both can be effectively managed.

The Measurements

Accepted measurements are used in evaluating each candidate money manager. Those most often used are the Alpha and Beta of a manager, the standard deviation and the Sharpe Ratio. The Alpha is the measure of a manager's excess performance relative to whichever index in which they focus their investments, then adjusted for the Beta. A positive Alpha means that the money manager is out-performing his index.

The Beta is a method of measuring the risk associated with a money manager. The Beta measures volatility in relation to the market index in which he or she focuses. The measurement is based around the foundation number 1.0. A Beta of 1.0 indicates that the manager's performance experiences the same ups and downs as the market, meaning that he or she is no more or less risky than the market. Any number greater than 1.0 means that the manager's portfolio is more volatile than the overall market in which it is invested, while a Beta of less than 1.0 indicates less risk than the index. It is important to also consider how the assets are invested when analyzing the Beta measurement.

Caution must be taken here because managers can alter their Beta numbers by placing some of their assets in cash or cash-equivalent investments, which lower the overall volatility of a portfolio, masking the existence of investments in high-risk securities.

The standard deviation of a money manager is similar to a Beta measurement, although it isn't quite the same. While the Beta measures against the overall investment market, the standard deviation only measures the performance of the single manager against him or herself. The higher the standard deviation, the more ups and downs a manager's performance experiences. The higher the highs and the lower the lows, the less appealing a money manager is because this relates back to his or her consistency.

The Sharpe Ratio measures the return of a manager per unit of risk. In this case, risk is defined as the standard deviation of the manager's return. Sharpe Ratios are most valid when comparing money mangers who invest using the same style and market capitalization. The accepted practice here is that the higher the Sharpe Ratio, the better the money manager, as it indicates a higher level of relative return for the incremental risk being taken.

The Sharpe Ratio analysis is one example of how a Molecular Consultant can assist in measuring managers at this stage in the selection process against their peers. Peer analysis is important for several reasons. Though a money manager has made it this far in the process; that is, he shows good numbers across the boards, has consistent returns, manageable risk, and high Alphas and Sharpe Ratios, he may not be all that he initially appeared.

It may be that with all of these positives, the money manager is, in fact, at the *bottom* of his peer group. What it means is he's just been investing in the right style and not doing so as well as the others. For example, if large cap growth is dominating the market and performing well, most managers who concentrate in that field will perform well, and because of that they will not have been filtered out by this point in the selection process. It is the peer group analysis against what everyone in that same field is doing that tells the tale. It is in this way that the Molecular Consultant can weed out the managers who are in the right place at the right time from the managers who are in the right place at the right time *and* are also great money managers.

Adherence

Another issue which must be considered is a money manager's adherence to his or her investment style. Some money managers may just be tactically reallocating their portfolios to follow market trends, which is exactly what nonprofits create Investment Policy Statements to avoid. Money managers who remain consistent in changing market conditions are those to whom a nonprofit will want to entrust the management of their portfolio.

This is one reason why you must pay close attention to how well a money manager performs in different market cycles. In a bull market a bad money manager can make himself look good by producing high enough returns to compensate for years of bad investing. And the opposite can also occur.

It is necessary to understand the big picture and not be blinded by misleading money manager performance reports. If a money manager stays true to his investment style and your nonprofit understands that downs will come on average about one-third of the time for very good managers when dealing with quarterly results, then you can understand how a money manager fits into your investment program. If a market goes down, then investments may go down, but the market, overall, has been rising since it existed. There will always be downs in the market in short-term scenarios, and it's the superior managers who prove their worth by performing well time after time relative to indexes.

If you're aware of this, you will be able to decide which money managers are the best. Selecting a money manager who reallocates outside of his or her parameters can result in a derailing of the established investment objectives. This is a potential that can be avoided by selecting appropriate money managers.

Operational Issues

This is another issue which is crucial in the consideration of money managers and their internal functions. The operational aspects of money managers can have a great deal to do with how they will perform in the future. One of the most important considerations is the retention of managers and officers. When you analyze any money manager you're actually analyzing the performance of several individuals. If the key investment staff of the management team have been employed by that firm for many years, it is likely that it was their work that is being measured when you analyze the performance of a manager. If the management teams are constantly changing, hiring and firing lead investment personnel you will most likely be analyzing the performance of someone who will not be managing your portfolio. Also, frequent changes in personnel in a money managing firm usually spell trouble.

It is for this reason that it is important to establish a continuity trail of performance to a specific money manager. If he or she is employed in a very successful house there is a tendency to assume he or she is responsible for that success, and you can be certain that is how it will be presented to you. But that might not be the case at all, so the Molecular Consultant will confirm that the specific money manager is taking credit for his own track record.

If a money manager outsources its research to the same sources employed by most of Wall Street then there is no advantage to that particular manager. For a management style that is uniquely successful, the money managers must be unique in their practices, including performing their own research.

Another reason why conducting in-house research is so important for money managers is because buying information from other people may make things easier for the money manager, but it can add to the overhead of their operation, which in turn will increase the fees and commissions to investors.

Also, finding money management firms in which the owners are invested is often a sound practice, because they have a stake in their managed portfolios and often have a tendency to outperform managed funds which are run by employees.

The size of the money manager and the length of time during which the manager has been operating are also very important considerations. A money manager who has many years of market experience is obviously preferred over one who is new to the industry and may not be aware of all aspects of asset management. Also, firms which deal in large assets often have advantages over smaller firms. If there is a lot of money with them and they have been around for a long time, it is typically true that they have deep investment talent and have proven that their money management is a winner.

Fees

It is never possible to know with certainty the future of any investment, nor can you know how effectively a specific money manager will perform. What you can know in advance is the fees you will be asked to pay.

Fees are no small issue and require special attention. Just as small incremental improvements in decision-making can have great rewards down the line, so too will a slightly higher fee at the start adversely affect the eventual rate of return. Some money managers are worth their fees, others are worth less than they want.

It is presumed that the money manager you select will deserve his or her fees; that is, that the money manager will bring such value to their portion of the portfolio that the fees charged will not seem significant. The law of supply and demand typically dictates fee level, and there is little you can do about that. The best at what they do, as is the case in any profession, tend to be paid the most, and as so often in life, when it comes to money managers you usually get what you pay for. But also keep in mind that there are no guarantees. A high fee does *not* assure you of a greater than average rate of return.

In most cases the fees charged simply come with the money manager. If you decide this is the individual you want, you take onboard the fee schedule that comes with the choice. If the nonprofit's portfolio is large enough, however, fees can be negotiable. This is a very specialized area and not one that lends itself to a quick study. The Molecular Consultant will either possess such expertise or will call on someone who does.

Many boards lean towards performance fees in the hope this will safeguard them from paying excessive fees for poor performance. It is argued that performance fees are the most fair because the money manager is compensated for his rate of return and in this scheme you do not pay significant fees for poor performance. But keep in mind that you only pay a lower fee if the rate of return is *below* the specified benchmark. In other words, you pay less when you haven't gained much. Considered in that light, they lose much of their appeal.

Performance-based fees are also subject to the criticism that they encourage risk-taking during a specific timeframe when the money manager has not done well. If during the grading period, say a quarter, the investments have fallen well short, the money manager will be under pressure to take on a greater risk in hopes of making a greater gain and recouping his losses. This is not an advantageous situation for the nonprofit. Upping the stakes is a quick way to lose in both gambling and the market.

The schedule for performance fees is also quite complicated. It must be thoroughly understood for many reasons, but perhaps the most important of these is that they will have the effect of driving investments. In other words, in such a complicated system the rules of the game, and perhaps not the best investment decision, can have the unintended consequence of deciding things. After all, this is how the money manager earns his or her living.

Before committing to a performance-based fee schedule, keep in mind that a money manager will be strongly motivated already to perform well. They understand that keeping your nonprofit as a client is dependent on their performance. They do not require artificial inducements to do their best.

Regardless of the system you ultimately employ with any money manager, the bottom line is that you be certain you know, in advance, *every* fee the nonprofit will be called upon to pay. This is not an area for surprises.

In addition to fees, the issue of trading costs should also be considered when evaluating money managers. The larger firms have more trading capability, which can lead to reduced costs on transactions which in the long run can make a significant difference on portfolio profits [or losses].

Selection

After these steps have been followed, you and your Molecular Consultant will have a concise list of several money managers which are very well-performing and able to meet the requirements of your nonprofit. From this list a series of presentations, interviews and careful evaluations will be conducted, the outcome of which will be to remove any of the money managers who have made it to this level of the selection process but are not qualified to manage your nonprofit's assets.

Your fiduciary goals will also have been met by making a prudent investment choice and allowing professionals with expertise and industry experience to take the reins of individual accounts in your portfolio. There are thousands of money managers and your nonprofit will have the ideal number and the best fit to successfully implement your IPS.

If the final decision is largely based on past perform-ance, or more specifically, on the degree to which the money manager has exceeded the established benchmarks for his or her investment class, it is generally taken that 3% above the benchmark, exclusive of fees, is "world class" performance. It is from such a relatively modest improvement over a benchmark that a portfolio will greatly profit. But it may very well be that the board will place greater weight on any or a number of the other factors that have been made available through the process.

And finally your nonprofit will make the selection and the nonprofit will have the ideal money managers for its needs. Risk tolerances will be satisfied. Asset allocation objectives will have been met, diversification of assets will have been accomplished and in time your return goals will be realized. You will grow your nonprofit to the next level as detailed in your Investment Policy Statement. The board of directors of your organization will have more time and resources to focus on the mission of your nonprofit.

The interesting aspect of this is that if the board has done its "homework" so to speak; that is, if it has prepared the Investment Policy Statement, performed an Asset Allocation Analysis and completed the other important steps *prior* to the actual money manager selection process, the individual picked often has less to do with eventual success than the fact that the preceding has already taken place.

But what it also means is that having done its homework, the board is far more likely to select the right person.

11.
DYNAMIC PORTFOLIO OPTIMIZATION

Modern Portfolio Theory has changed everything when it comes to portfolio management.

The concept was first advanced in the 1952 paper, *Portfolio Selection*, written by the renowned Dr. Harry Markowitz. For the first time it was possible for investors to estimate anticipated risk and the rate of return, and to measure both with statistical reliability. From this came a methodology for constructing portfolios to optimize market risk against anticipated gains, making clear that while risk is intricately tied to return, it can be managed within acceptable parameters. This was not only a novel concept, but quite revolutionary.

Markowitz demonstrated how to create a properly diversified portfolio and conclusively showed that such a portfolio was likely to perform well. He proved that in equal circumstances the portfolio with *less* volatility would outperform one with *greater* volatility. To one degree or another, modern portfolio management has its origins in these architectural principles.

Before MPT

Prior to Modern Portfolio Theory it was accepted practice for investors to focus on assessing the risk/return characteristics of the individual investment vehicle they were considering. The investment approach was to locate those vehicles that offered the best likelihood for reward with the least element of risk. A portfolio was then constructed from these. On its face this sounds perfectly sound and that's why it was the philosophy employed for so many years.

But in such a system it was possible, and often occurred, to construct a portfolio entirely from a single class of investments. This happened because individually, each met the desired standard. Instinct suggested, however, that this was not a wise approach. Though each on its own looked good, the same economic factors could adversely effect each of them and hence the investments overall. But it was feared that spreading investments about, just for the sake of covering all bets, would produce poor results.

What Markowitz did was to devise the mathematics of what came to be called the "diversification effect." He mathematically demonstrated that investors were better served by focusing on selecting a *portfolio* with the desired risk/reward characteristics they sought, instead of compiling a list of vehicles individually with those characteristics. He demonstrated with a high degree of accuracy that a sound investment policy was about the portfolio and not the individual investments. This change in emphasis was profound in its impact.

Modern Portfolio Theory

At its core, MPT is a mathematical approach for determining the optimal asset allocation for an established degree of risk. To accomplish this Markowitz required you first establish the rate of return, devise the standard deviation of various returns, then put in place a method for evaluating and monitoring the investment vehicles, often called a matrix. His mathematical equations then calculated asset allocations which had the lowest standard deviation from the projected rate of return. In other words, it showed how to invest with the least amount of risk.

The consequence is that Modern Portfolio Theory provides a vast backdrop against which to understand the various interactions of return and risk that are systemic to all investments. It has utterly changed how every institution, including nonprofits, manages their portfolios. It is the force behind passive investment techniques as well as the various mathematical models that are today extensively employed in managing risk and assessing potential gain.

Perhaps the single most important consequence of Modern Portfolio Theory is the accepted investment principle that you must surrender perceived safety and assume a measure of risk to receive better returns. Markowitz showed the relationship between risk and return, and demonstrated how to maximize return with the lowest level of acceptable risk.

Prior to this no such correlation was understood to exist. In fact, risk was to be avoided if at all possible. The idea was to find that magical investment with great return and *no* risk [if possible], then put all your eggs into that basket. Markowitz's concept of managed risk changed everything.

Markowitz's theory was advanced by the work of others over the coming decades. In general, it came to be agreed that it was possible to construct an optimal portfolio which provided the greatest return for *any* established level of risk. The essential concept is that investments should be monitored, measured and managed at the portfolio level, not investment by investment. Investment vehicles should ideally be selected not on their individual merit alone, but rather on their place in the balanced portfolio.

Problems with MPT

As revolutionary as Modern Portfolio Theory proved to be, over time certain shortcomings became apparent. They are generally agreed to be:

1. ***The lack of a standard methodology to establish the key data input.*** This meant that every money manager, or other analyst, who claimed to be following MPT could devise his or her own creation by skewing the incoming data. Even adhering to the prevailing industry standards of the time was, in fact, nothing more than following the latest trend.

2. ***The timeframe became skewed and unreliable.*** The information initially relied on in establishing a portfolio through MPT is traditionally grounded in monthly and quarterly timeframes. But in MPT the analysis is reduced to a matrix, deviations and averages, and these are not usually tied to the customary timeframe investors rely on.

3. ***MPT is a buy and hold model.*** As traditionally formulated, MPT does not allow the kind of routine adjustments that are now possible through our more sophisticated market analysis and technology. In essence, you establish a portfolio and hold onto it until you perform another MPT review. It simply lacks the flexibility that is now possible and, because it does, limits opportunities for marginal rate of return increases that can significantly mount over time.

4. ***Normal distribution must be followed.*** Any deviation from normal distribution in a MPT devised portfolio causes the asset allocation to skew. Again, it limits what has come to be regarded as standard flexibility in managing a modern portfolio.

Advantages of Dynamic Portfolio Optimization

During the long decades since *Portfolio Selection* was first published, there have been many improvements on Modern Portfolio Theory and practice. Our understanding of the markets and of investment strategy has advanced considerably, and we today possess far more tools with which to analyze financial forces than ever before. There are a number of new investment management systems, but perhaps the most effective has come to be generically known as Dynamic Portfolio Optimization. This strategy has been demonstrated to provide a greater rate of return than more traditional models wedded to Markowitz's 50-year-old model.

As DPO has been increasingly recognized for the advantages it brings to the traditional MPT portfolio, several of these are of significance. DPO should:

- Consistently outperform the MPT models.
- Increase the probability that you will avoid a bear market.
- Make it more likely to discover those factors impacting your portfolio.
- Provide an overall greater rate of return.

In addition, investors employing DPO tend to have greater confidence in their portfolio. Because of that they are less inclined to make decisions for psychological reasons or to direct ill-advised and resource-consuming reviews and reports.

Characteristics of the Post-MPT Portfolio

As resources and tools for financial investment increased in sophistication after the 1950s, the limitations in Modern Portfolio Theory began to assert themselves. It became apparent over time that it was possible to do a better job in creating a portfolio strategy and in managing the portfolio itself. There are various approaches to accomplishing this, but each seeks to "optimize," that is, to maximize the rate of return while maintaining the same degree of risk.

To accomplish this, changes from the Markowitz model were necessary. These have included:

- Prevent distribution from skewing asset allocations.
- Limit the number of initial inputs needed to construct the portfolio.
- Automatically update the inputs.
- Allow an alternate form of risk assessment.
- Establish traditional timeframe references of months and quarters.
- Create a more flexible, or dynamic, structure which allows altering the asset allocations as needed.

Systems for permitting these changes have long existed and have well-established track records of performance and reliability. One key principle for optimizing a portfolio is that the underlying anticipated rate of return for any investment vehicle will influence its value.

This is not as complicated as it may first seem. It simply means that the dividend you anticipate a stock receiving affects the value of the stock. This is true for every investment in the asset allocation, though it is not always that easily calculated.

This is simply another way of saying that each vehicle has a relative, rather than a fixed, value. And because relative values are always changing, opportunities are routinely coming available.

The Efficient Portfolio

In Modern Portfolio Theory you limit, and in effect control, volatility by diversifying your risk among the various classes of investment vehicles. This is enhanced by adding to the mix the investment styles of the money managers. In this way you can assemble a portfolio with a defined measure of risk, but the overall risk to the portfolio is less than for any one of the vehicles. In other words, volatility tends to cancel itself out while still producing a higher than benchmark rate of return.

In this model, diversification is more a factor of how the various vehicles perform one in relation to the other than compared to the actual number of vehicles held. The principle behind diversification is to have vehicles with various characteristics. The concept is that as they are not interrelated they will tend to balance against one another.

The objective is to create what is called an Efficient Portfolio. This is defined as one that provides the greatest gain for an established risk level. It is possible, in fact, to chart a line which connects the efficiency factors and visually demonstrates the degree of efficiency inherent in such a constructed portfolio.

The Mean-Variance Model

In Modern Portfolio Theory the standard approach is to establish the optimal asset allocations by basing them on investment return averages, the standard deviations derived from them and various correlation coefficients. These have been set by relying on historical patterns of performance. This mean-variance model, however, has four serious considerations:

- Using standard deviation as a measure of risk.
- The impact of certain return distributions.
- The large number of inputs that must be estimated.
- The absence of a logical procedure to generate expectation inputs over an extended timeframe.

Dynamic Portfolio Optimization, as an extension of the traditional Modern Portfolio Theory, addresses these con-

cerns by providing:
- A downside risk measurement in place of standard deviation.
- The downside risk measure that deals with the problematic return distributions.
- Asset allocation that is directly tied to certain influencing factors such as interest rates, political concerns, etc. to obtain the most desirable mix.
- An alternate system which significantly reduces the number of inputs.

The effect of these changes is to create new points as to when and how to adjust asset allocations. In this way, DPO provides a reliable navigation tool to manage the modern portfolio.

Dynamic Asset Allocation and Market Timing

Some investors rely on market timing as the key component in managing their investments. They will switch most, even all, of their portfolio from stocks to bonds when the circumstances appear right, then back again when they change. History proves this to be an exercise in futility.

Dynamic asset allocation constructs a portfolio with more than two investment vehicles. It guides the investor in rebalancing the portfolio among the established classes. Such effective movements are essential for a more productive portfolio.

Consider the situation when it comes to the periodic rebalancing that every portfolio undergoes. The most common method is to simply return the portfolio to the percentages provided in the Investment Policy Statement. The investment strategy might be to have a portfolio balanced with 60% stock, 35% bonds and 5% cash equivalents. Most money managers would simply blindly return to those numbers when a rebalancing point is breached. What he or she would be ignoring are the lessons of behavioral finance. People, even institutions, tend to behave at certain times with a herd mentally. This is also one of the reasons why all investment vehicles have a relative value. At such times, these relative values can mean that a certain asset class is under or overvalued. These are opportunities, opportunities the traditionally constructed and managed MPT portfolio cannot exploit.

Responding to such opportunities is not the result of instinct, but is rather the consequence of well-established and detailed analysis with tried and tested methodologies. The Molecular Consultant will either be knowledgeable about these or know the expert to consult who is.

What comes from this is tactical modeling. That is, though investments remain within the established parameters, a determination is made as to which assets are over or undervalued and the rebalancing is made with that taken into account. In the above example, the IPS would allow a range of percentages for stocks, say 50% to 70% instead of simply 60%. This allows for a more significant change in this asset class based on the knowledge of current market conditions and the relative value of the vehicles.

These methodologies in Dynamic Portfolio Optimization permit the exploitation of gain opportunities provided by market inefficiencies. They tend to be incremental and not dramatic, but applied systemically over time they add significantly to the portfolio's rate of return.

12.
INVESTMENT PROGRAM ANALYSIS

Once the investment strategy is in place and the portfolio decisions have been made and put into action, it is then necessary to monitor and analyze what is occurring. Regardless of the superior nature of the overall investment program, monitoring is required to assure that it stays as intended and is responsive to the nonprofit's needs. This must not be an *ad hoc* procedure or one that takes place only when there is a perceived problem because by then it will almost certainly be too late and lead to ill-advised decisions.

Once again, this is about process, the established process designed to monitor every meaningful aspect of portfolio management in a routine manner. By monitoring and evaluating a number of significant variables, the Molecular Consultant will usually anticipate problems sufficiently in advance to allow a more productive response by the board or nonprofit management. With a proper system in place, decisions will not be made by impulse or in a state of perceived crisis.

Monitoring is just that: monitoring. It is meant to raise issues for review, but the results of monitoring will not always require that any action be taken. The primary purpose of monitoring is not to compel action, but rather to provide relevant information in a timely manner. It is the long lead time this makes possible that gives effective monitoring its great strength.

A monitoring process is designed to accomplish at least two objectives:

- Identify issues that might have an adverse impact on the portfolio and investment strategy.
- Provide the relevant information so that issues can be properly evaluated and a suitable course of action, if any, can be undertaken.

Even with an outstanding Investment Policy Statement and superior money managers onboard, there always exists an element of uncertainty about any portfolio. It is simply the nature of financial markets and of investment decisions that this is so. It is, unfortunately, not possible to eliminate all worry. But an effective monitoring program will help enormously in minimizing the degree of concern the board will typically experience, especially during a volatile market period. It should allow timely answers to important questions and unexpected concerns.

Having the necessary information about the portfolio during times of stress can provide a great deal of assurance. Decisions made in such a circumstance are far more likely to be beneficial over the long term. Knowing you have a process in place that assures you will get timely information is the best hedge against uncertainty any board can reasonably expect.

Characteristics

A systematic portfolio and money manager monitoring system will possess certain specific features that ensure the board will routinely receive the information it requires to perform its duties. In most cases that information is provided quarterly. It will include detailed reports and charts designed for monitoring your specific investment strategy, investment performance and portfolio activity.

In addition to occurring at least quarterly, these characteristics will include:

- Account monitoring.
- Money manager monitoring.
- Relevant benchmarks for comparison.
- Information to facilitate comparison with appropriate benchmarks.
- An overview of the existing market conditions and performance statistics for peer investments and groups.
- An evaluation from the Molecular Consultant relating to the relevant collected data.

The Procedure

In most cases, though not always, the report and accompanying evaluation will be prepared directly by the Molecular Consultant. As he is unaffiliated with any of the money managers the board is assured that he is acting impartially.

Before the board receives this information and these reports, the Molecular Consultant will have analyzed them as to overall rate of return. He will also have examined the various affected components. These he will have compared against the specified investment objectives and the parameters which were previously established.

The evaluation will analyze single-money-manager accounts and combined accounts with several money managers. Comparison of money managers will be made side-by-side so the board can appropriately evaluate performance. The evaluation will also facilitate comparisons of various money managers responsible for different aspects of accounts. The previously established benchmarks, or, where appropriate, historical benchmarks, are integral in allowing the evaluation of the relative performance of the various money managers. In evaluating style, performance and risk, the benchmarks are the yardstick.

Also compared is the performance of an individual money manager to that of a group of money managers with a similar investment style. Such information is key in putting a specific money manager's performance in proper perspective when compared to existing market conditions and peer performance.

Once all the information is collected, the Molecular Consultant will provide his evaluation to the board along with the underlying information itself.

First Steps

The individual overseeing the monitoring and the preparation of the reports and accompanying evaluation, usually the Molecular Consultant, will begin with a careful review of the existing Investment Policy Statement. He is primarily concerned that it adequately states the objectives for each account within the portfolio in terms of risk and anticipated return. He will review the nonprofit's spending policy to determine if it is realistic. He will consider the designated investment styles, asset allocation, benchmarks, and the set standards of evaluation, both for accounts and the money managers. He will determine if the IPS is consistent, comprehensive and whether its assumptions are both realistic and attainable. If the IPS is found to be wanting, then he will make specific recommendations to the board to correct it.

Next, he will perform a review of the account's structure which will include both style and asset allocation. This should allow him to conclude if the investment program is consistent with the anticipated rate of return and degree of risk tolerance. He will then determine if the investment strategy is efficient in terms of providing an adequate mix of investment styles. Again, if there exist any shortcomings he will make specific recommendations to correct them.

This is followed by a comprehensive review of each money manager and their accounts, with emphasis on the various investment styles. There is a comparison of their past performance to what is now taking place. Particular attention is paid to diversification of the overall account. From this an initial impression is formed as to whether or not the current mix of money managers and various investment vehicles contributes to placing the total portfolio in conformity with the objectives of the Investment Policy Statement. Again, specific recommendations will be made, if called for.

The process includes a review of the various custodial and brokerage arrangements and the fees associated with them, as well as the costs overall. These will be considered as they compare to the current market and industry standards. Alternatives will be explored, if appropriate. And once again, recommendations will be proffered, if required.

Monitoring Accounts

From inception, individual accounts will be monitored. Though much of this can be conducted internally, there will be occasions when the process could include the board and the money manager. There are three services relating to accounts that must be performed on a routine and regular basis.

First, each month, each account must be reconciled to ensure accuracy. The reconciliation will focus on every item that impacts the account's market value. It will include the current position, cash flow, transaction activities and fees. The information will be carefully scrutinized for omissions, inconsistencies, errors or peculiarities. All disparities will be adequately examined and a resolution reached. The necessary data from all this is then entered into the reporting system's database for use in the next quarterly report.

Each quarter a detailed set of reports on investments is prepared which examines every significant aspect of each account. Copies are provided to the board and any others in the nonprofit's management who should have them for review and consideration. The Molecular Consultant will then meet with the board or its designated representative for such matters, if any, to discuss the performance of the various accounts. It may well have been that he met with the representative at different times during the quarter as issues came up. But he will also meet directly with the board to discuss the report and his evaluation.

As part of his responsibilities, the Molecular Consultant will have conducted his own internal review of all accounts at least each quarter. He may draw on the expertise of certain consultants as needed. He will monitor each account's performance in light of the established parameters and make a note of inconsistencies or abnormal patterns. He will document his analysis. All of this will go into his evaluation which accompanies the quarterly report to the board.

Each year the Molecular Consultant will reexamine the nonprofit's Investment Policy Statement, review the allocation of every account and its market position, as well as any changes in investment practice that may have occurred during the year. At an appropriate time he will meet with the board and discuss whether modifications to the IPS should occur. If that is agreed, he will draft a formal modification for adoption and inclusion.

Monitoring the Money Managers

As important as is keeping an eye on the accounts, it is just as important to know the performance of the various money managers. It is routine for the Molecular Consultant to deal directly with each money manager on various aspects of his or her performance to facilitate the monitoring process. In such an approach the due diligence of monitoring money managers evolves as a joint responsibility of both the Molecular Consultant and board.

Each money manager is periodically asked to confirm the accuracy of the information maintained about him and his company. He will also be asked to provide his most recent promotional materials, fee schedules and management agreements. Such requests are often accompanied by a letter asking that each money manager answer a series of questions about any events or changes that may have an impact on the money manager.

Each month, if variances between the parameters and the account's position are observed by the Molecular Consultant, he will provide them to the money manager for correction. If they persist, he will contact the money manager, usually face to face, to discuss the continuing discrepancy. One avenue of discussion will be to consider if the parameter requires adjustment in light of the current market. If that is the case, the issue will be discussed with the board or its representative. If not, the money manager will advise of the steps he or she intends to take to bring the account back into compliance.

On a daily basis, if required, the Molecular Consultant will discuss with the money manager any issue concerning investment issues that have come up in order to reach an agreement on what should be done. In these cases, timely action usually produces the most positive result.

Finally, before the Molecular Consultant meets with the board on an account, he will have consulted directly with the appropriate money manager. While due diligence is always an aspect of their relationship, it is most effectively obtained in a cooperative environment and one in which regular communication takes place.

The Benchmarks

The purpose in establishing benchmarks as part of the investment strategy is to provide a yardstick against which to measure the performance of asset classes and money managers. It often occurs that other historical benchmarks must be compiled to allow proper monitoring and evaluating of money manager performance.

Benchmarks permit analysis to take place on a relative basis. Benchmarks form an integral part of the report on money manager performance, as they do on the performance on style and of asset classes. Benchmarks not already established are determined by analyzing a specific money manager's investment style along with the investment goal of the accounts. These must be properly balanced.

The analysis of a money manager's investment style has two components which should result in a consistent form of measurement:

- Examination of the core data of specific investment vehicles that the money manager has in his or her average portfolio.
- Examination of the related coefficients tracking the performance between the various performance measurements and the money manager's historical performance.

A certain benchmark may have but one index or it might be composed of a blend of several. This can mean tracking hundreds of indicators. In addition, every account will have total return benchmarks. In an account balanced with different asset classes, say equity and fixed income, each will be assigned its own specific benchmark. The overall account, however, will receive a benchmark that has been custom designed and which reflects the account's target asset allocation. It should be noted that such a customized benchmark is *not* routinely rebalanced so it accurately reflects the existing asset weighting. This allows a comparison between the produced results from the investment strategy and the actual asset allocation.

In addition, it is necessary to have a benchmark for each matching portion of the portfolio. There will be a primary benchmark against which the money manager's performance is evaluated. There will also be a reference benchmark that is usually composed of a wider index and is not ordinarily specific to any certain investment style. Its purpose is to allow comparison of the money manager's performance against the broader market. There will be other benchmarks, such as one to measure inflation, which is of particular use in evaluating the bond portion of a portfolio.

The types of benchmarks and their number will vary from account to account even within the same portfolio as they must reflect the money manager's style and goal of each specific investment account.

Peer Group Analysis

While comparing a specific money manager's performance to a commonly accepted benchmark is of great value, it is also highly desirable to compare his or her performance against that of the peer money managers who administer similar accounts in related nonprofits. This peer group pool will also possess the same, or very similar, investment styles, and will match favorably with the style-specific indicators previously selected to be his or her account's benchmark.

In forming a peer group pool, the data relied on is taken from composite performance figures provided to commercial databases by various money managers. Only money managers who have reported their historical gross investment performance for at least the last five years are considered. This assures that the information is current and that data exists which can be applied for the comparison. This data is used to select for the pool those money managers who are favorably matched. This is an extensive process often involving more than 1,000 money managers in 4,500 investment composites. Individual performance composites are then divided into asset classes. Each asset class is subdivided into more specific groups which can be employed for comparison.

Once this has been completed, performance is then calculated for each money manager grouping within the pool. In addition, a calculation is made for all of the money managers, who are then ranked from highest to lowest each quarter. This provides the actual metric against which the individual money manager is compared.

Investment Style

The money manager was retained with the expectation that he or she would manage the assigned account with a certain style, so evaluating a money manager's performance against investment style is essential. It will reveal if he or she is buying investment vehicles consistent with his or her history and stated style. It will also allow you to know if the money manager is remaining within the indicated investment parameters. Deviation from the style can, and usually does, impact diversification, investment risk and attainment of the account's objectives.

In examining a money manager's investment style, the first approach is Holdings Based Analysis. This relies on the basic, or fundamental, characteristics of the specific vehicles that are in the account. In the case of equity securities, these include price, earnings ratio to price, book ratio and price, cash flow ratio and the like. Duration, quality and maturity are considered in the case of fixed-income vehicles such as bonds.

Each of these variables is then analyzed compared to matching averages in a comparable segment of the market in general. Fundamental Analysis disregards gains that are the result of the overall account and a composite of all of the individual vehicles.

The second approach is called Return Based Analysis. This approach relies on the historical investment performance previously garnered. In other words, how does the previous rate of return compare to the rate of return for the current investment style? Return Based Analysis disregards the basic characteristics of all of the account's individual investment vehicles.

Though quite different, both of these analyses are important in determining how the individual money manager is positioning his account within the portfolio and how the portfolio itself is placed within the market as a whole. It is possible, however, that each approach may produce a very different answer. They can agree, or not. The significance is not that they agree or disagree, but rather that they raise appropriate issues which should be considered and possibly brought to the attention of the affected money manager.

The Evaluation

The right mix of money managers is essential to the proper performance of the portfolio. The wrong mix will almost certainly lead to a failure to meet the targeted rate of return. But replacing money mangers when it isn't called for is also disruptive and creates its own set of problems, not the least of which is increased expense unrelated to better performance. For these and other reasons, the evaluation of money manager performance must be comprehensive, fair and informative.

The Molecular Consultant will gather as much relevant information as possible and draw comparisons where they are called for. The purpose isn't to give a specific grade score or to point the board towards a single decision. What is intended is to collect and present what is needed so issues requiring attention are identified in a manner that allows a timely and meaningful decision. As is often the case for the individual in reviewing a private portfolio, the review itself is all that is required. In other words, if the earlier steps properly occurred, the periodic review as a result of monitoring will generally not require that any significant action be taken.

The review and evaluation also serve an important function in assisting the board to fulfill its institutional and individual fiduciary responsibilities. The Molecular Consultant assists by providing an accurate, detailed, and, most of all, an objective report on every key aspect of money manager performance. It is such a monitoring process that contributes greatly to confirming the earlier decisions.

13.
NONPROFIT INVESTMENT
TOOLS & TACTICS

Because it is so heavily regulated and provides certain tax advantages, the nonprofit community is quite complex, both for the operation of a specific nonprofit and also for donors. Nonprofits have many vehicles through which contributions can be received. Various giving plans offer different opportunities to nonprofits and donors, but they also can restrict nonprofits in significant ways.

How the relationship between a donor and a nonprofit is arranged has a profound impact on the success of a gifting program. It is important that a professional who is familiar with all of the gifting tools available to nonprofits and nonprofit donors guide boards through the process of determining which are best suited for their nonprofit and donor needs.

The Case for Planned Giving

There are many different ways to give. Each has its own merits to a donor and each can assist the nonprofit in a different way. An individual may wish to consider a charitable plan for giving that will dovetail with their estate and financial planning. In this way, he or she will derive from their charitable gift other benefits such as additional income, or reduced income, gift or estate taxes.

Most charities accept gifts in a variety of forms so that prospective donors may choose the types of gifts that are most efficient, personally satisfying, and financially advantageous for themselves and the nonprofit. There are a wide range of gifts which can be given to a nonprofit and many reasons why one is employed rather than another. There are a wide range of rules and regulations that govern the tax benefits as well as the deductibility values and property values of gifts, so a qualified tax expert should always be consulted prior to making a charitable gift.

Gifts

A gift of cash is the most commonly used means of giving. Gifts of common stocks, bonds, mutual funds, or other appreciated securities may be made. Depending on the circumstances, the securities will either be managed or liquidated to achieve the donor's goals. A popular benefit of such a gift beyond the charitable income tax deduction is that, in most cases, capital gains tax on the appreciation of the securities can be avoided. Gifts of real estate and many other properties of value may be given as well. These gifts often receive the same tax treatment as gifts of securities; that is, no capital gains tax plus deductibility at fair market value.

Many companies match the gifts their employees make. If the donor's employer has a matching gift program, his or her gift to a specific area of support may be doubled or even tripled. If the donor's company has a matching gift program, the Human Resources Department at the company will be able to provide additional details and a matching gift form.

Deferred Gifts

Gifts can be immediate or designed to be given at a later time. Deferred gifts are contributions that cannot be used until some future date. Deferred gifts are the result of careful planning that integrates the donor's charitable gift with his or her overall financial, tax, and estate-planning objectives in order to maximize the benefits for both the donor and the nonprofit. Every deferred gift is closely regulated by law and requires special arrangements and tax treatment.

The Current Gift

Current gifts are contributions that can be put to use by the nonprofit immediately on receipt. It is also a donation made directly to a nonprofit by a donor. This gift can include nearly any asset though typically gifts of this type include cash or checks, stocks, bonds, commercial property, personal property, art, antiques, or even cars. The only process involved here is the transfer of ownership from the donor to the nonprofit.

These types of gifts are often straightforward, but occasionally a gift will come along that might not be wise for a nonprofit to accept. For example, the gift may be hard to sell, or may contain hidden problems. The gift might be a house which has a leaking oil tank, or a major donor may donate art that is ugly, offensive or both. A gift acceptance policy should be crafted detailing precisely what kinds of current gifts your nonprofit is allowed to receive.

The Charitable Lead Trust

With the charitable lead trust the charity receives income from the donor's assets for a specified period of time, after which the asset is transferred back to the donor or to the donor's heirs. A lead trust can reduce gift and estate taxes or provide a charitable deduction for the donor.

In a charitable lead trust payments are made annually to a nonprofit, or any number of nonprofits, for a specified number of years. When that timeframe is up, the remainder of the trust is paid to non-charitable beneficiaries as provided in the details of the trust. Often this provides for the remainder to be paid back to the donor or to the donor's family. Trusts that pay back to the donor are grantor charitable lead trusts. Trusts that distribute the final assets to beneficiaries other than the donor are known at non-grantor charitable lead trusts. Such a trust provides tax advantages to the donor while, in most cases, permitting him or her in time to distribute a measure of his or her wealth to family members.

While a donor can create a grantor or a non-grantor charitable lead trust, the donor has a choice to select the character of the income being distributed to the charity. He can either choose to create a charitable lead annuity trust or a charitable lead unit trust.

The Charitable Gift Annuity

One planning vehicle which is used by nonprofits to receive contributions is a charitable gift annuity, or CGA. A CGA is organized by the nonprofit rather than the individual donor. In this case a donation is made to the charity and in turn the charity makes annuity payments to one or two life annuitants. A portion of the annuity payment may be income-tax-free, and an income tax deduction may be allowed for the difference between the value of the gift and the present value of the annuity. In broad terms it's a two-step process, including a charitable gift followed by the purchase of a fixed income annuity contract.

In this case, the charity takes on more responsibility which comes in the form of a general obligation to make the annuity payments *regardless* of the value of the fund. In the other planning vehicles if the value of the fund reaches a point at which distribution to donors is not possible, then it simply isn't done, just so long as that eventuality happens for legitimate reasons. With a CGA, however, the charity assumes responsibility to pay the annuity amount regardless of contributed assets. The charity becomes in essence a basic insurer, acting much like an insurer in a commercial annuity.

The difference, however, between a commercial annuity and a charitable gift annuity is the gift aspect. This in turn affects the annuity rates, causing them to be lower, so as to allow for the gifting component.

There are many issues which must be considered when deciding to create a CGA. Most nonprofits should take into account the size of their organization and their mission. There is a large amount of work associated with a CGA. If a nonprofit is small and doesn't possess the infrastructure to manage the process and assume the risk behind a CGA, then this planning vehicle should not be implemented.

Types of Charitable Gift Annuities

There are two basic types of CGAs, both related to the annuity payments:

- Immediate obligation
- Deferred obligation

In an immediate obligation annuity the charity is required to make payments from the first year on a fixed payment schedule and continuing at a set frequency. A deferred gift annuity is an annuity in which the distribution of annuity payments is deferred for at least one year from the inception of the contribution.

Within these two are many variations. The beneficiaries of the annuity can be single or joint and last for the lifetime of the individual or individuals involved. The recipients in a joint annuity are often husband and wife, or sometimes children.

There is a lengthy process involved in determining the annuity rates, which is dependant on many factors. The starting date must be determined and factored in and there are provisions to be considered. A formula must be applied, then compound interest factors must be multiplied in. The process can be rather math intensive at times.

Charitable Gift Annuity Advantages and Benefits

Like all charitable donation planning vehicles there are tax benefits to charitable gift annuities. In their use there are three issues which typically arise:

- The calculation of charitable contributions in the form of income tax deductions.
- The method in which annuity payments are taxed.
- How to recognize any gains made by the donor during the transfer of property as per the considerations of the annuity agreement.

The CGA planning vehicle is one that offers many advantages to donors and nonprofits, and should be considered by all organizations. A CGA, for example, does not require that a separate agreement be drafted for each donor. This means that smaller donation investments are more feasible for nonprofits with a CGA. A charitable gift annuity can also attract more donors because it allows for the donation of debt-burdened property. Because the gift annuity technically isn't a trust, it avoids the regulations which prohibit trust funds from accepting debt-encumbered property as donations.

Of course, there are any number of regulations and rules which govern the drafting of such plans, but in certain situations, if this plan is right for your nonprofit, the benefits will outweigh the costs. However, the nonprofit should be sensitive to the need to invest gift annuity assets properly. Since the charity acts as the grantor of the funds it is liable for the stream of income for the life of each annuitant regardless of the rate of return earned.

The Charitable Remainder Trust

Charitable remainder trusts are versatile tools to generate income for the donor or other beneficiaries while reducing or avoiding taxes. It pays the lead interest to the designated non-charitable beneficiary, then distributes the remaining interest of the trust *after* the other beneficiaries have been paid to the charity. It is important to note that a non-charitable party is the target of one distribution during a specified period in a specified amount.

There are two types which vary in their payment amounts in charitable remainder trusts: annuity trust or unitrust. An annuity trust makes payments based on a fixed amount which does not and cannot change until a time specified in the trust. A unitrust is a payment amount based on a percentage of the value of the assets of the trust which are to be revalued at least annually.

A charitable remainder trust must make distributions for either a predetermined number of years or during the life span of an individual or individuals. Charitable remainder trust law limits percentages of annually distributed assets. The annual pay out must be a minimum of 5%, and a maximum of 50%, of the initial net value of trust assets valued either once at the inception of the fund [an annuity trust] or valued annually [a unitrust].

The charitable remainder trust is governed by explicit requirements set forth in statute which specify what is required of a trust to meet IRS standards. If the charitable remainder trust doesn't qualify, and failure to meet just one of the requirements can affect qualifications, then *all* tax deductions are void. It's an area that requires expertise.

There is also a Charitable Remainder Annuity Trust, or CRAT. A CRAT may be funded through a gift of stock, cash, or other assets. This type of gift provides for a predictable, fixed life-long income for the donor and his or her beneficiaries. No additional contributions may be made to a CRAT, however, additional annuity trusts may be established. The donor may claim a tax deduction for the estimated proportion of the assets that will ultimately go to charity.

A Charitable Remainder Unitrust, or CRUT is very similar to the CRAT. The trust provides yearly, fluctuating income to the donor or his/her beneficiaries for a specified number of years, or for life. Additional contributions may be made to the trust, and upon the death of the last beneficiary, the nonprofit receives the principal and uses it in accordance with the donor's wishes. The estimated remainder is tax deductible.

Three Original Unitrusts and Their Characteristics

Unitrusts share certain characteristics in common. Each has an irrevocable charitable remainder at the end of all individual income interests, income payments to individuals can be annual, quarterly or monthly and the minimum pay out percentage is 5%, the maximum 50%. In addition, the present value of future charitable distributions must be at least 10% of the initial funding value, and following any additions. This requirement should be taken into consideration when drafting testamentary funding of a unitrust.

Each type of unitrust, however, is distinguished by a different way of determining dollar payments of the income interest. The three original versions are:

- Standard Charitable Remainder Unitrust [referred to as Type I, or STAN-CRUT]
- Net Income Only, Plus Make-up Unitrust [referred to as Type II, or NIM-CRUT]
- Net Income Only Unitrust [referred to as Type III, or NI-CRUT]

Dollar payments to individual income recipients of a standard unitrust *must* equal the specified pay-out percentage of annually predetermined asset value. There is a "four-tier" structure of sources from which the trustee must make up the payments: first, from ordinary income earned; second, if that is not sufficient, from past realized capital gains; third, from "other" income [i.e., tax-exempt income]; and fourth, from principal if required [also untaxed]. Dollars received from each tier retain for recipients the taxable nature of their source. The same required amount and four sources of payment also apply to annuity trusts.

Payments from the net income only, plus make-up and the net income only unitrusts *do not* use the four-tier method of meeting the stipulated pay out percentage each year. Trust agreements state that in any calendar year payments to recipients shall be *the lesser* of ordinary income earned and the stated maximum percentage payout. Generally, realized capital gains are added to the principal, unavailable for payments, and all payments to individual recipients are taxable to them as ordinary income, although the trust document can change this.

Stan-Crut vs. Nim-Crut or Ni-Crut

The primary reason for use of the net income only, plus make-up unitrust [Type II] and the net income only unitrust [Type III] is to preserve the principal of the trust in any year in which ordinary income earned is not sufficient to cover the stated percentage of asset value. This can be particularly critical when a unitrust is first funded. Time may be required to sell an asset in order to reinvest and meet the income payments required. Funding assets that usually require a Type II or III unitrust are real estate with uncertain marketability, and low-yielding stock in a company with excellent long-term prospects.

When the facts of a situation suggest that sale and reinvestment can be accomplished, but not in time to provide cash for early required payments, enough cash or readily marketable stock can be added to the initial funding to provide sources for early payments. Another option for a standard unitrust funded early in a calendar year is to specify an annual payment at the end of the year, allowing more time to achieve liquidity.

Nim-Crut vs. Ni-Crut

When these options do not provide sufficient assurance for meeting the payments of a standard unitrust, either the Type II or Type III is available. In past years, the Nim-Crut has been the more frequent choice, with its provision that any shortfall in a year between ordinary income paid and the maximum permissible percentage shall be noted and remains *subject to make-up payments* in any subsequent years when ordinary income exceeds the specified pay out percentage.

There are situations, such as when life income recipients have a relatively long life expectancy, the Type III NI-CRUT *without make-up* provision may be preferable. Until the underlying property is sold and proceeds reinvested for a higher return, the grantor-recipients have essentially the same pre-tax income as previously received from the property, and improved after-tax income following use of the charitable deductions created. This also avoids the temptation to invest eventual sale proceeds for higher fixed income to cover make-up payments, thus foregoing the potential for long-term growth in value and dollar payments.

The "Spigot" Unitrust

Another application of the Type II Nim-Crut has been to provide supplemental retirement income for the grantors, sometimes termed a "spigot" unitrust. Typically the grantors enjoy high income while fully employed, and fund a make-up unitrust with growth stocks paying little or no dividends, or with cash that the trustee similarly invests. Trustees can shift the investment objective from growth to higher yield when the grantor-recipients need improved income, including make-up payments.

This use of unitrusts has come under scrutiny by the Internal Revenue Service, following some aggressive examples it termed "accelerated" and considered abusive of the original concept. The 50% maximum annual pay out rate and minimum 10% charitable remainder value for all CRTs are efforts to meet this concern. On the other hand, the technique also increases the eventual charitable remainder for the benefit of society, and should remain an option when used in the best interest of all parties to the trust.

<u>Payment Format</u>

The payment format of a charitable remainder trust can also be an important decision for donors. In order to determine which form of donor payment is best, there are a number of factors to consider:

- The marketability, liquidity and the ability to produce cash flow from the assets of the portfolio.
- The goals and risk tolerance of the nonprofit beneficiaries.
- The donor's goals regarding the end sum of the charitable gift.

It is important that the donor and trustee be aware of the type of assets in the fund. An asset which is not liquid, such as real estate, may create issues when payments are due from the property. If a distribution isn't made, for example, because a property can't be sold, then there is a chance that the amount of the unitrust or annuity will have to be included in the gross income portion of the donor's tax statement.

The income goals and the risk tolerance of the nonprofit receiving the donation are also important considerations for potential donors. Just as there are risk tolerances in investment vehicles, there are also risk tolerances associated with the various types of trusts. With a charitable remainder trust there is an inherent prospect that a loss of capital can occur. This will create a disparity between the percentage of the assets being paid out verses the pay out rate as defined by the trust.

For example, consider a trust fund with $1 million at its inception, $100,000 of which is to be paid out yearly to a designated nonprofit. If the market value of the fund declines, say by 15%, than the market value of the fund drops to $850,000, causing the $100,000 required annuity payment to become a relatively higher pay out. At the inception of the fund, the distribution was 10% of assets per year. But after the depreciation of the fund by market forces, it would still be paying out the same $100,000 but that is now nearly 12%.

This is the kind of risk that can be associated with the various planning vehicles available to donors. The unitrust plan, however, avoids this risk in this example by readjusting the distribution amount downward in the event of a market value drop in the assets of the fund.

Selection of Payout Rate

The most important decision in this planning process is the selection of the annuity trust or unitrust pay out rate. There are formulas used to determine pay out rates based on the various investment vehicles in the trust. The deductions are based on the remainder interest in the trust. This is made up of eight factors:

- The net market value of the fund.
- Whether the trust is in an annuity trust or unitrust format.
- The annuity or pay out rate.
- The timeframe of the trust [number of years, lives of income recipients or a combination]. The older the individual the higher will be the charitable deduction.
- Frequency of payment.
- In the case of the unitrust, the number of months

between the valuation date and payment date.

- In the case of an annuity trust, whether the payment is at the beginning or the end of payment periods.
- Applicable Federal Mid-term Rate [AFMR].

Once these factors have been considered, the proper annuity or unitrust rate can be established, which will in turn determine the tax benefits available to the donor.

Comparison of Charitable Trust Benefits

There may be comparative differences between the income tax charitable deduction for a CRUT and a CRAT. Take the example of a couple both aged 70, who have a $1,000,000 stock portfolio with a cost basis of $500,000. They would like to receive an income pay out of 6% each year. If they created a CRAT they would receive $60,000 annually and their upfront income tax charitable deduction would be $302,830 [based upon an IRS Discount Rate of 5%]. If they created a CRUT, their income would be variable based upon the value of the assets of the trust as valued each year, but their income tax charitable deduction would be significantly higher, $359,410 [based upon an IRS Discount Rate of 5%].

The Charitable Lead Annuity Trust

A charitable lead annuity trust distributes a fixed amount at least once every year based on a percentage of the initial value of the trust, a predetermined sum, or a formula which trust executives employ in order to create specific, desired tax breaks. As this amount is predetermined, it is independent of the actual performance or interest gains of the trust. The amount cannot be redefined at any point during the life of the trust unless it is specified at its inception, in which case the time must be specified as to when the annuity value may be changed. In some cases this can lead to problems for the donor, because if the trust cannot afford to make the predetermined annuity payments, then the trustee will be compelled to invade *corpus* to obtain the annuities to be dispersed.

The Charitable Lead Unitrust

The other form of charitable lead trust is a unitrust. It is very similar to the charitable lead annuity trust, the difference being that rather than provide for a fixed amount, the payment to the trustee is a fixed *percentage*. The percentage is based on the market value of the trust, which can be reassessed at any point, so long as it is at least once a year.

These two forms of charitable lead trusts are very common ways for donors to gift money to nonprofits. The charitable lead unitrust allows donors to make additional contributions during the life of the trust while also providing them the opportunity to name one or more non-charitable beneficiaries, including family members or even the donor. Gifts are eligible to be deducted against as much as 30% of the trust's contribution base. There are several rules which limit potential abuse of such trusts, but nothing that shouldn't be expected. For example, the deduction taken from a trust cannot exceed the value of the assets in that trust.

The primary reason for creating a charitable lead trust is to reduce taxes, create a stream of income to a charity for years and to defer the receipt of assets. For example, an affluent family may create a non-grantor charitable lead unitrust or annuity trust when children are young so that the children can receive the assets when they are mature adults. By establishing the charitable lead trust the parents can reduce or eliminate gift taxes. The grantor charitable lead trust can help reduce income taxes the year the trust is created or any unused income tax charitable deduction can be deferred for an additional five years. Interestingly, in a grantor charitable lead trust the rules require distributions to charity over the life of the trust to be taxable as income to the grantor. This is known as "phantom income" and a tax expert should be consulted to determine if this is an appropriate strategy.

The only charitable lead trusts which possess tax exemption are qualified ones. Plainly put, a non-qualified charitable lead trust will be subject to gift or estate taxes and its estate, gift or income taxes cannot be deducted. There are an extraordinary number of exceptions and rules which control the governance of charitable lead trusts, too numerous to mention. Surprisingly, there are no actual guidelines which specify what it takes to qualify a charitable lead trust, but there are a number of rulings which planners and drafters use as guides to assure that their trusts will receive a favorable determination. In most cases, it is possible to obtain an advanced ruling on the qualification of a trust.

There is also an expansive set of rules which govern the various ways in which unitrust and annuity trust can or must be paid out. The two basic distribution options are standard income and net income. The net income option was designed to alleviate pressure on trustees who may have to invade the *corpus* when trust funds do not have sufficient means to make established unitrust distributions. It allows for distributions to be based on net income, thus over-paying the unitrust distribution. This is known as a "make-up" which is used while following a net income unitrust distribution plan.

It is also possible for a trust to have a flip option which allows a charitable remainder trust to change from a net income unitrust to a standard unitrust. This can be very important for donors in certain situations. For example, a donor may create a charitable remainder unitrust funded with a gift of real estate. The real estate may not provide sufficient income to pay the income beneficiary until the real estate is sold so the net income provision is necessary since the trust will only be able to provide whatever income is earned from the real estate, if any. Once the real estate is sold, the trustee can convert the net income unitrust to a standard unitrust.

There are many variations of charitable lead trusts and charitable remainder trusts, and within these variations exist numerous governing rules and regulations, along with many exceptions to them. There are advantages and disadvantages to both types of trusts and many considerations to be taken into account when dealing with these gift-making planning vehicles.

Comparison of CLAT and CLUT benefits in a Non-Grantor Lead Trust

For a family considering establishing a non-grantor lead trust the gift tax charitable deduction between CLAT's and CLUT's may be different. Take the example of a couple that is contemplating either a CLAT or a CLUT with a term of 15 years, contributed principal of $1,000,000 with a cost basis of $500,000 and a pay out of 6%. If they selected a CLAT their gift tax charitable deduction would be $634,360 verses a gift tax deduction of $593,220 for a CLUT based upon an IRS Discount Rate of 5%.

A Word about Trustees

The role of the trustee of a charitable trust is to prudently invest, administer and manage trust assets, provide income distributions, provide tax reporting and, upon termination, distribute the assets. The trustee has a duty to both income and remainder beneficiaries. An individual, bank or trust company can act as a trustee. In some states the charity itself can act as a trustee. This is a heavily detail-oriented task and as you approach these situations you must determine if the individual, nonprofit, bank or trust company has the experience to manage trusts of this type.

The Pooled Income Fund

A very different planning vehicle through which nonprofits can receive donations is the pooled income fund, or PIF. Unlike the charitable trust funds, the PIF is created by the nonprofit, rather than the donors. A PIF can be created through the creation of a pooled income fund trust agreement, it can be thought of as a funnel through which the funds for donors are pooled and then placed directly into the assets of the nonprofit. In this situation, the donors are typically individuals, each of whom is assigned what is known as a "unit of participation." This is a percentage of the fund that their individual contributions comprise.

These units of participation are used to determine the percentage of distributions which are paid out. These distributions are made annually and for the lifetime of participants. After death, the funds attributed to that donor are severed from the pooled income fund and used for charitable purposes.

The advantage of participating in a PIF is that any assets contributed into the fund qualify for charitable income, gift and estate tax deductions. The amount of the deductions allowed is based on the value of the remaining interest in the trust. This form of donation is often a means for donors to avoid payment of capital gains tax on any appreciated property which is transferred to the fund.

There are, inevitably, rules and regulations to govern pooled income funds. They provide that each donor must transfer property, thus contributing an irrevocable amount of remaining interest in such property to or for the use of the nonprofit, and retaining an income interest for the life of one or more beneficiaries who are alive at the time of the original transfer.

In a PIF the property must be commingled with property transferred by other donors who have made or are making similar transfers. The PIF must not include security investments which are exempt from taxes. All funds in the trust must meet these requirements without exception.

It is also required that every beneficiary receive income based on the interest of the funds of the trust once a year determined by the rate of return earned by the trust for the year. To qualify as a PIF, the trust must meet every requirement and any relevant IRS rulings or procedures. The IRS will also not provide advanced rulings as to whether a transfer to a PIF qualifies for charitable income, gift, or estate tax deductions, though the IRS will rule regarding any provisions that deviate from those found in the sample documents published in the Revenue Procedures.

The Molecular Consultant will be familiar with this type of fund and these issues. Though he is not a tax expert, he will be able to advise whether or not a PIF is a worthwhile goal for your nonprofit.

Most nonprofits which fit the description to qualify for a PIF are religious organizations, educational institutions, hospitals, medical education and research organizations, and foundations which are based around communities. Any privately operating foundation or supporting organization is explicitly excluded from participating in pooled income funds, with the exception of private operating foundations which fit the IRS description of public charities because those nonprofits may be considered for income tax deductibles as well.

If a nonprofit ceases to exist, for any reason, while a PIF is still funded, the donors must choose an alternative, and qualified, nonprofit to which their funds will be transferred.

A PIF also has several maintenance requirements. The nonprofit towards which the fund is directed must be in control of the funds. This can be performed directly by the nonprofit, or managed indirectly much as a Molecular Consultant would do for a nonprofit which decided to participate in a PIF.

PIF Income Distribution

The distribution of the income from a PIF can be a very tricky subject and requires careful planning on the part of the nonprofit and its professionals. Every beneficiary of a PIF is compensated by means of a *pro-rata* share of the total rate of returns earned by the investments of the fund during the taxable year. The value of each *pro-rata* share is determined by dividing the value of assets by the number of shares outstanding. This means that the value of the shares oscillates with any additional transfers of property into the PIF as it affects the appreciation or depreciation of the fund's fair market value.

This measurement is taken on what's known as a "determination date." The determination date is defined, simply, as the day on which the market value of a fund is measured. A fund must be valued at least four times a year. The first of these must be the first day of the taxable year, and there can be no more than 3 months between any of the other measurements.

The payment frequency, which must be at least once annually, is taken into consideration during the planning process. In most cases, however, portions of the income per unit are distributed every quarter. There are several mechanisms which govern the payment frequency of income funds; however, no matter what the frequency of payments there is no effect on the computation of deductions for income, estate or gift tax purposes.

Pooled income fund's payment distributions are limited to ordinary income items such as dividends and interest. PIF cannot distribute realized capital gains. For that reason many PIFs primarily utilize income-producing investments.

Measuring the Term of Payments

Related to frequency of payments is the term of the

payments. The period of the relationship between an income recipient [the nonprofit] and the fund is based on the life of the individual who contributes to the fund. It is the allowed uses of these interest incomes by the donor that often prove problematic. The donor has several options, including:

- Retaining the income interest for the remainder of their life.
- Designating payments to other individuals [so long as they are living when the contributions are transferred to the fund, and can include a class of beneficiary].
- If income is paid out to more than one beneficiary, then paid concurrently or consecutively, or any combination of the two.
- The instruments which govern these payments must include specified timing of payments.
- Retaining partial income interest for him or herself and pay other portions to one or more other individuals.

<u>PIF Implementation</u>

There are also rules governing the implementation of Pooled Income Funds. They must be officially declared through the use of a master trust agreement, both established and executed by the nonprofit maintaining the fund.

The means through which a donor enters into participation in a PIF is known as a Vehicle of Transfer. This is a document which details the date of the transfer, the number of beneficiaries, the portions of income payable to each individual income recipient and the methods for how each will be paid, the right of the donor to revoke a non-donor income interest, and finally the ultimate use to which the remainder of the interest shall be put, i.e. for what charitable purpose/purposes.

There is another requirement which is placed on PIFs by the Securities and Exchange Commission. This requirement involves the inclusion of a disclosure report which provides potential donors with a complete disclosure of the processes and procedures of the fund. The disclosure statement of a PIF came about as the result of several investigations. In 1972 the SEC stated that it will not take action against Pooled Income Funds if:

- The PIF is qualified to receive tax-deductible contributions.
- Each potential donor has received a written disclosure document stating the procedures for the operations of the PIF.
- Those soliciting contributions are volunteers or an employee involved in the nonprofits fund-raising efforts.
- No solicitor receives compensation based on the amount transferred to the pooled income fund due to his or her fundraising work.

A PIF is run like any other invested account and must face the challenges and decisions which other funds face. These issues include asset allocation, which is dictated by the objective of the fund. Most PIFs are composed of a managed security portfolio, constructed with fixed income investments and equities for income and capital appreciation of the fund's assets. However, with different needs come different asset allocation requirements, such as more complicated investment tactics like hedge funds or real estate investment trusts.

Another form of investment found in PIFs is what is known as a Real Estate Pooled Income Fund. This consists of a fund which invests in real estate with the intent of using it for the needs of the charity. This is frequently employed by PIFs created for colleges and universities or medical and research facilities. These organizations often accept gifts in the form of property, liquidate the property, and than use the profits from liquidation to upgrade already existing facilities or to construct new facilities.

Advantages of the PIF

There are many advantages to using a pooled income fund. One is that there's no need for the donors to draft any documentation for the trust because everything has already been set in place by the Vehicle of Transfer. Even though most donors will have all documents carefully reviewed by their professional advisors, it makes the workload involved with their contributing much, much less.

Another significant advantage is that only a single tax return filing must be done. Unlike charitable remainder trusts, a PIF only requires that a single return be filed by the nonprofit, regardless of the number of individual donors who participate in the fund.

Another advantage which helps the PIF attract a greater number of donors is that they can accept smaller donations than a charitable remainder trust can. The reason is that a PIF has the economic ability to diversify their investments and still meet minimums by having strength in numbers. That along with the fact that there is much less administrative work associated with a PIF makes it relatively easy for them to accept relatively small donations. This in turn allows generous individuals who may not have the means to make large donations in the form of trusts to participate in contributing to charities.

What also attracts more donors is that the income distributions are not at all age sensitive. Everything is equal in a PIF, regardless of age. This is not the case with all trusts. Pooled Income Funds also don't have the minimum remainder interest that CRTs do in order to qualify.

There are many advantages, as well as many nuances, involved in Pooled Income Funds. A Molecular Consultant will be able to advise you through the process of determining whether a PIF is a planning vehicle which will benefit your nonprofit in ways which other vehicles may not be able to.

Other Types of Contributions

In addition to those previously discussed, there are other forms of gifting which can also be considered:

1. *Bequests [Will or Living Trust].* The most common form of planned giving, a bequest, is made through a will or living trust. Bequests may be stated as a percentage of the estate, as the residual of the estate, or as a specific dollar amount. Since a will can be changed, no income tax benefits are associated with a bequest. However, the owner's estate is reduced by the amount of the bequest for estate-tax purposes.

2. *Deferred Gift Annuity.* A donor makes a gift now and receives an immediate income-tax deduction. However, in this instance the donor begins receiving the annuity payments at a future pre-determined date. Due to the compounding of the gift's income, the amount of the annuity payments can be significantly greater than the annuity payments under the charitable gift annuity.

3. *Retained Life Estates.* A donor may transfer the ownership of a personal residence or a farm, while retaining the right to live there for the remainder of his, or her, life. The donor will be entitled to a charitable income tax deduction for a portion of the appraised fair market value of the property at the time of the transfer. In addition, the donor escapes capital gains tax on the property's appreciation and the estate will be entitled to a charitable tax deduction.

4. *Retirement Accounts.* A donor may name a charity the beneficiary of the account with the value being fully deductible for estate-tax purposes.

5. *Life Insurance.* Charities can be named the beneficiary of a life insurance policy to create a gift of much greater value than the actual money paid by the donor. A donor may contribute a "paid up" policy to the charity and receive an income tax deduction equal to the policy's

cash value. Or, a donor can name the charity as the beneficiary of the policy resulting in estate-tax savings. Or, a donor can name the charity owner and beneficiary of a new policy and receive an income-tax deduction for the premiums paid.

The planning vehicles just discussed are very commonly used by donors and nonprofits in the charitable contribution world. Understanding them is extremely important, but beyond these very intricate types of giving there are many other ways in which individual donors can contribute to nonprofits.

There are many options when it comes to the planned giving of individuals to nonprofits. The decisions involved in determining how to obtain donations from your donor pool in such a way as to *expand* your donor pool, *increase* donations and keep donors *happy* is not an easy one. It is, however, very important to most nonprofits.

A Molecular Consultant will be knowledgeable on all of the various planning vehicles. The world of nonprofits is facing many changes and to successfully meet these challenges every nonprofit will need the support of its donors. Creating the proper planning vehicles and being able to meet donor needs is the best way to accomplish that.

CONCLUSION

Nonprofit consulting and investment guidance is as much art as science. Every nonprofit has its own unique DNA – in its organization, in its mission, in its fundraising and in its portfolio.

Whom you elect to work with is at least as important as the investment strategies and portfolio management practices you adopt. In fact, it can be argued that the consultant is more important since you rely upon them to deliver strategies and practices you will follow.

We have attempted here to provide an overview of modern investments for nonprofits, but also to reveal the unique ways in which a Molecular Consultant can serve you. He can bring a unity and coordination in expanded fundraising and investment that is often lacking. His unique skills and experience in Demographic Analysis and Behavioral Finance, as well as other important areas, bring a new dimension to any nonprofit in this first decade of the 21st century. We believe it is not too much to say that the Molecular Consultant can change the very ground on which a nonprofit stands. The changes can be that profound.

We are entering the age of the modern donor. Over the next 25 years an estimated $41 trillion will become available for contribution to nonprofits. The modern donor has different expectations than did the traditional donor. He or she wants to know they are making an impact. They are also less trusting and demand transparency from the nonprofits to which they give or are considering giving to.

These are unsettling times for all public institutions in America. The Sarbanes-Oxley Act has had a profound impact on publicly traded companies and its requirements are slowly spreading into the nonprofit community as well. There has never been a time when greater demands have been placed on every type of nonprofit.

The events of 9/11 changed our world and temporarily altered traditional giving patterns. Other crises will occur with similar disruptions. These and the advent of the modern donor compel that the responsible nonprofit act now to conform its operation and investment strategy to the new equations of the 21st century.

What is upon us is an enormous opportunity. The economic engine of America has produced an unprecedented degree of wealth, a large portion of which will be directed to helping the missions of today's nonprofits. Positioning yourself to take advantage of this opportunity should be the primary objective of every nonprofit.

It is in this new world where the Molecular Consultant can be of greatest value. He understands what must be done. There is, really, no time to waste. Every day a nonprofit stands still is a day further it has fallen behind.

BIBLIOGRPAHY

AMERICAN PHILANTHROPY. Robert H. Bremner. Chicago : University of Chicago Press, 1988. 2nd edition.

Traces the history of philanthropy in the United States from the 17th century through the 1980s. Includes a timeline of important events in American philanthropy from 1601 to 1987 and a bibliography of suggested readings.

ARE WE READY? : SOCIAL CHANGE PHILANTHROPY AND THE COMING $10 TRILLION TRANSFER OF WEALTH. Michael May. Washington, D.C.: National Committee for Responsive Philanthropy, 1999.

Includes the following chapters: A rainbow of community funds; Payback time for women's groups?; Coming out...as donors; Inspired donors make giving an art; The next generation; Passing the plate and feeding the spirit; The Fidelity Gift Fund says Have It Your Way; Support advocacy : call your mom!

THE BIG FOUNDATIONS. Waldemar A. Nielsen. New York, N.Y.: Columbia University Press, 1972.

A 1972 study of the 33 largest foundations in America by a former Ford Foundation official, this book includes information on their history, financial expenditures, and influence on society.

BUILDING THE WORLDWIDE COMMUNITY FOUNDATION MOVEMENT. Ottawa, Ontario, Canada : Community Foundations of Canada, 2000.

Reports on a 1998 conference held in Miami as well as examines the development of the movement to increase the number of community foundations in the world. Also provides a brief history of this growth in the U.S., Caribbean, South America, Europe, Middle East, Central and Eastern

Europe, Africa, and Asia and the Pacific.

INVESTING IN PENSION FUNDS & ENDOWMENTS: TOOLS AND GUIDELINES FOR THE NEW INDE-PENDENT FIDUCIARY. Russell L. Olson, New York. McGraw-Hill, 2003.

> A commonsense guidebook for producing superior pension management returns – without sacrificing fiduciary responsibilities.

MANAGING YOUR INVESTMENT MANAGER: COM-PLETE GUIDE TO SELECTION, MEASUREMENT, AND CONTROL. Third Edition. Arthur Williams III, Chicago. Irwin Professional Publishing, 1992.

> An indispensable resource for those managing large pools of other people's money. Helps to improve communication between fund sponsors and investment managers.

THE TRUSTED ADVISOR. David H. Maister, Charles H. Green, Robert M. Galford, New York. Free Press, 2000.

> A very readable book that will be welcome to the inexperienced advisor and expert alike.

THE ARTFUL JOURNEY: CULTIVATING AND SOLIC-ITING THE MAJOR GIFT. William T. Sturtevant, Chicago. Institutions Press, 1997.

> Relationship building to obtain major contributions.

THE ART OF TRUSTEESHIP: THE NONPROFIT BOARD MEMBER'S GUIDE TO EFFECTIVE GOVERN-ANCE. Candace Widmer, Susan Houchin, San Francisco. Jossey-Bass, 2000.

> How to fulfill ten key trustee responsibilities with much-needed detail.

BUYING A MOVEMENT: RIGHT-WING FOUNDA-
TIONS AND AMERICAN POLITICS. Washington, D.C.:
People for the American Way, 1996.

Examines the funding patterns of a number of significant
conservative foundations and their grantees. Demonstrates
that conservative foundations have developed a
comprehensive funding strategy, providing grants to a broad
range of groups with each promoting right-wing positions to
their specific audiences. Includes bibliographic references.

*Foundation Management Series, 10th edition, Vol. I -
Finances, Portfolio Composition, Investment Management
and Administrative Expenses in Private Foundations /
Council of Foundations, 2001.*

Details trends in investment management practices and asset
allocation in the first book of a three-volume set.

*Investment Management for Endowed Institutions / L.B.
Siegel, The Ford Foundation, 1999.*

A guide to investment decision-making and asset allocation
for organizations with funds intended to be used over an
extended period of time or preserved and grown for future
use.

*Spending policies for foundations : the case for increased
grants payout / P. Mehrling. - San Diego : National Network of Grantmakers, 2000.*

Payout by private foundations and public charities is the
source of funds from which flow the grants that support much
of the non-profit activity in the United States. This report
offers a broader perspective on foundation growth - including
investments, gifts, and new formations - painting a picture of
philanthropic finances with a lesser emphasis on endow-

ments. Among the topics dealt with in the text are grants payout, foundation growth, and perpetuity and payout. Full contents listing is provided.

Sustainable payout for foundations./ Grand Haven: Cambridge Associated, Inc., 2000.

A study evaluating the sustainable real level of payout for private foundations in light of the actual experience of a sample of private foundations with diversified portfolios located in the State of Michigan.

Managing a private foundation / P.K. Rhoads. – Washington, DC : The Philanthropy Roundtable, 1999.

A follow up to the publication 'Starting A Private Foundation.' Aims to discuss the activities and responsibilities of a private foundation manager. Topics covered include: long-term planning, trustee organization, staff, investments, grants management and day-to-day decision making.

Community foundation training manual : III - management. - Washington, DC : Council on Foundations, 1990.

Third in a series of six manuals looking at the various aspects for creating and running a community foundation. Practical guidelines are offered throughout the series which together cover mission, governance, management, resource development, grantmaking and communications and public relations. This particular volume addresses planning, legal dimensions, structure and organization, administration, supervision, finance and networking.

Calculations within this document are for illustrative purposes only and should not be considered legal, accounting, or other professional advice. Individual prospective donors should consult their tax counsel.